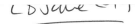
PAY ME FORTY QUID AND I'LL TELL YOU

The 2015 election campaign
through the eyes of the voters*

who largely ignored it

Michael Ashcroft & Kevin Culwick

Biteback Publishing

First published in Great Britain in 2015 by
Biteback Publishing Ltd
Westminster Tower
3 Albert Embankment
London SE1 7SP
Copyright © Michael Ashcroft and Kevin Culwick 2015

ISBN 978-1-84954-977-6

10 9 8 7 6 5 4 3 2 1

A CIP catalogue record for this book is available
from the British Library.

Set in Adobe Caslon Pro by Soapbox, www.soapbox.co.uk

Printed and bound in Great Britain by
CPI Group (UK) Ltd, Croydon CR0 4YY

CONTENTS

ABOUT THE AUTHORS

Lord Ashcroft KCMG PC is an international businessman, author and philanthropist. He is founder and chairman of the board of Crimestoppers, a member of the board of the Imperial War Museum and a trustee of the Imperial War Museum Foundation, chairman of the Trustees of Ashcroft Technology Academy, chancellor of Anglia Ruskin University and treasurer of the International Democrat Union. From 2005 to 2010 he was deputy chairman of the Conservative Party. His political works include *Smell the Coffee: A Wake-Up Call for the Conservative Party*; *Minority Verdict*; *Project Blueprint*; *What Future For Labour?*; *What Are the Liberal Democrats For?*; *It's Not You, It's Them: Research to Remind Politicians What Matters*; *Degrees of Separation: Ethnic Minority Voters and the Conservative Party*; *They're Thinking What We're Thinking: Understanding the* UKIP *Temptation*; *Small Island: Public Opinion and the Politics of Immigration*; *Europe On Trial and Cameron's Caledonian Conundrum*; and *Call Me Dave: The Unauthorised Biography of David Cameron*. His research is published in full at LordAshcroftPolls.com.

Kevin Culwick has been the director of Lord Ashcroft Polls since 2010. He was formerly head of opinion research for the Conservative Party, having previously worked in the polling industry and in politics. He plays the piano a bit.

*To Anna and Samuel, whom I missed
when on the road, and to the Guerrilla Moderator,
for unrelenting insight and good company.*

KC

INTRODUCTION
Lord Ashcroft KCMG PC

The 2015 general election produced the most unexpected result in Britain's recent political history. Polls in the final weeks suggested the contest was too close to call; the final surveys completed the night before voting, including mine, had it as a dead heat. The decisive Conservative victory was a shock to the polling world.

But the numbers are only part of the story. From the beginning of 2015 until the election, Lord Ashcroft Polls conducted regular focus groups all over the country to find out what undecided voters made of it all: what they had noticed and what had passed them by; how the leaders were coming across; what they thought the parties were trying to tell them and how believable (or otherwise) they found it; what mattered to them and what didn't; which way they were leaning and the doubts that stopped them making up their minds; and what they hoped or expected the outcome to be.

Write-ups of the groups were published every Monday on my website and on Conservative Home, alongside the results of the weekly Ashcroft National Poll, which was based on 1,000 telephone interviews. It quickly became clear that the focus-group findings were more interesting – and told us more about what was really going on – than the numbers. The reports acquired something of a cult following, and several readers were kind enough to suggest they should be compiled as a book. Here it is.

It would probably be too much to claim, even in retrospect, that the focus-group discussions pointed unambiguously to the election result that ultimately came to pass. But certain things were clear. There was no enthusiasm for Labour, even among people who were quite fed up with the coalition; there was none of the yearning for change that was evident in 2010, let alone 1997. The general view, as expressed by one of our participants with characteristic pith, was that "David Cameron's pretty good, but Ed Miliband is a muppet". If people had yet to feel the benefits of the economic recovery they kept hearing about, at least things seemed to be going in the right direction, while Labour showed no signs of having learned the right lessons from having been booted out five years earlier. They never won people's confidence on the economy, or, specifically, the public finances: yes, they might spend more on the health service, but all the money would be borrowed – or, as a chap in Wolverhampton put it, if the Labour Party were a house, the furniture would be nice but it would all be on HP. In Scotland, meanwhile, the rise of the SNP as a distinctive political voice heightened the perception that Labour and the Tories had simply become "different shades of shite". Though even its own supporters conceded that the SNP voting in Westminster on matters devolved to Holyrood would amount to having "two pies at the same time", south of the border there was indignation in the final weeks at the idea of the party having a big say in the government of a country it did not even want to be part of.

This would all seem to point to a comfortable victory for the Tories. So why did we not see it coming? Because other factors were at play. Many people were torn between two alternatives or were altogether undecided. The things that had held the Conservatives back in the past and helped prevent them winning a majority in 2010 – most importantly, doubts that they were really on the side of ordinary people – had not gone away. And in many Liberal Democrat seats, the formidable reputation of incumbent MPs continued to count even with voters unimpressed with what the party had achieved in government. These considerations lent plausibility to the polls that showed Labour and the Conservatives neck and neck.

Whether the nation resolved its collective dilemma at the last minute or whether the Tories had it in the bag all along is a question the polling world continues to grapple with. We may never know the answer for sure. But, in future elections, I expect the upshot of the Great Polling Debacle of 2015 to be a more circumspect approach to bare voting intention figures and a greater focus on the bigger picture. The kind of research whose results are described here has a huge part to play in that.

Indeed, one of the reasons these focus-group reports captured the imagination of readers was that they offered an extra dimension to political coverage. They also served as a rebuke to the depressing tendency to over-interpret individual polls or small changes between one survey and the next. (After I published some new figures last year, one of my Twitter correspondents asked, in all seriousness, whether the fieldwork had been done before or after the shadow Communities Secretary had attacked Waitrose for giving away free coffee.) I might also add that the gratifying reaction to this work proved how exotic ordinary electors were to parts of the commentariat.

This book, then, describes the 2015 election campaign as it was seen, not by its protagonists, but by its audience: the voters. The findings were captured by Kevin Culwick, the director of Lord Ashcroft Polls, who (in an effort as heroic as his expenses claims) travelled to thirty-three constituencies for sixty-six focus groups for discussions lasting a total of ninety-nine hours and involving over 500 people.

Above all, I think the reports collected here show that although most people do not follow every storyline in the political soap opera – they have better things to do – nothing very important gets past them. On election night, before the polling stations closed, I spoke at an event and stuck to my policy of not making predictions. Instead, I observed that the British people "are good judges of character and they don't believe the unbelievable. Whatever they have decided today, I'm sure they knew what they were doing." I defy you to read what follows and disagree.

MAA
July 2015

OPERATION ROLLING THUNDER
Kevin Culwick

For people involved in politics, the first experience of observing a focus group often induces both horror and fascination. The fascination comes from seeing how normal, everyday people react to the kind of questions that occupy the political operative's every waking hour. This is also what causes the horror.

The first reason for this is that in the political operative's world – dominated, as it can easily become, by an endless succession of minor crises concerning matters of next to no real importance – normal, everyday people can be something of a rarity. Many of those who work in politics professionally, or who write about it for a living, spend most of their time with people like themselves, or with each other.

The good ones realise the dangers of this and make sure they maintain a broader perspective, but for some, the exposure to normal people can sometimes come as a shock. A few years ago, after we had spent an hour listening to eight middle-aged men in the East Midlands complaining grumpily about immigration and the cost of petrol while displaying no signs of having noticed any of the Tories' dazzling recent initiatives – standard focus-group fare at the time – a high-flying member of the party's creative team asked me, "Why are they *like* that?" Like what? "Well, like *that*. Is it the kind of media they consume?" To her, these ordinary blokes were as mysterious and forbidding as Komodo dragons.

Elected politicians themselves are somewhat less quarantined, having constituents to contend with. Indeed, most MPs are probably more in touch, as well as harder working and better intentioned, than their voters would give them credit for. But some of them have a tendency to romanticise their role as tribunes of the people. Sometimes they paint a picture of their electors as simple, salt-of-the-earth types whose outlook on life can be easily grasped, as in the case of the MP who likes to claim that it is not possible in his constituency to buy an olive. They can also be prone to thinking that casual conversations in their "patch" give them all the insight they need into popular sentiment.

But the average Member of Parliament represents 70,000 voters. They cannot help but be most in touch with their own supporters and activists, or those who need assistance, or have views about forthcoming legislation, or otherwise have the time and inclination to contribute to their mailbag or inbox. As Gyles Brandreth put it, recalling his own time in the House of Commons, MPs tend to meet two types of people: "Those who have problems and those who are right."

This means MPs are most likely to be struck by the second big lesson focus groups have to impart, which is that most people do not give politics a thought from one month to the next. It can be dispiriting, to say the least, for politicians to realise that hardly anybody notices most of what they do. Unless and until they transgress, that is; duck islands last longer in the memory than any number of well-judged speeches in the chamber.

The first time one (then) shadow minister came to an evening of focus groups, he had spent much of the preceding weekend in broadcast studios giving interviews on a story that fell within his brief. He was eager to hear what people had to say about his performance. Not only could our participants not remember the story – let alone his part in it – they could barely think of anything the party had said or done for months. This kind of trauma does politicians no lasting harm, and helps them to keep things in perspective.

The same can be true for the third lesson, which is that the way parties and politicians sometimes conduct themselves can be terribly counterproductive (a truth so obvious to most people that they would wonder at the idea that research might be needed to explain it). Here I have something of the zeal of the convert. Before I started to work in polling – and had the equally epiphanous experience of getting a job outside Westminster – I spent long days in the Conservative "war room" helping to come up with the kind of stories that seemed a triumph at the time but which I now know, and ought always to have known, make newspaper readers turn the page with a disdainful sigh. I literally shudder to think of some of them. In the early days of opposition after 1997, we decided, almost certainly unjustly, that the new Labour ministers were enjoying the trappings of office rather too liberally, and that this ought to be brought to the voters' attention. The ensuing delivery to 10 Downing Street of a gold-sprayed foam pig on a pedestal – the "Snouts In The Trough Award" – probably represents the pinnacle, or nadir, of our efforts. I wish I were making this up.

Focus groups show in unambiguous terms what people think of politics as it is too often practised, and how they feel about politicians of all persuasions who seem to come from similar backgrounds with similar advantages and appear to treat the whole thing as a game. The message can be so stark that politicians sometimes leave determined to do everything differently. Yet the bad habits can be so ingrained that this resolve often lasts only as long as the journey back to Westminster.

For some, focus groups stand for everything they dislike about contemporary politics, and, indeed, much of modern life: superficial, looking only to the short term, a sorry substitute for principle and conviction. Used wrongly, they could be all of those things, but that is not what they are for. They are not supposed to tell politicians what to say or do or think. Done properly, they are an honest attempt to understand what people think and why. That does not make their findings any the less exasperating for those who do not like, and consequently do not want to hear, what they have to say.

Shortly before the 2010 election, another (then) shadow minister lamented what he felt was the low calibre of ammunition being supplied to him by Conservative HQ: he wanted to be able to deploy, in every interview, six snappy but devastating sound bites that would remind people exactly what to think of the Labour government. Oh, people hate all that, I reminded him. It makes them roll their eyes and switch off. They know what they think of Labour, they're just not sure they want to vote Tory instead. "The trouble with you," he mused at length, "is that you spend too much time in focus-group land."

But research does not take place in a different realm. There is no focus-group land, only voter land, and people involved in politics need to know how things look there. To complain that a party pays too much attention to focus groups is to wish it would stop thinking about the electorate.

*

Despite their value as a barometer of opinion, and as a reminder of who the audience is, what they have noticed and what they make of what they see and hear, the use of focus groups in the media has been comparatively rare. This presented an opportunity for Lord Ashcroft Polls. As part of our work on the 2015 general election, alongside the data we produced in our national and constituency polling, we decided to hit the road and find out whether the parties' frenetic campaigning was having any effect on the people it was supposed to impress: undecided voters in marginal seats.

As well as getting a good geographical spread – urban and rural, towns and suburbs, from Cornwall to Scotland – we made sure the destinations we chose reflected the local political battles: Tory against Labour, Liberal Democrats against either, UKIP possibilities and, in one memorable week, a taste of the SNP surge.[1] Recruiters were despatched with their clipboards to find the right people: in each location, eight men and eight women who had voted at the last election – half for the sitting MP – but had not decided which party to support in 2015. Suitable targets were offered £40 as an incentive to turn up on the appointed night. Indeed, despite what their participants might think, focus groups are probably the only place in British politics where cash really does change hands in brown envelopes. (At the end of each group, as likely as not, someone would ask the moderator whom he or she intended to vote for. The inevitable reply: "Pay me forty quid and I'll tell you.")

---

1. In the interests of transparency, which is the hallmark of Lord Ashcroft Polls, I should point out that our choices of location were subject to certain additional considerations having to do with logistics and, not to put too fine a point on it, catering. Anywhere south of Birmingham and east of Bristol could be covered by car in one night. Beyond these boundaries, hotels had to be selected. Whatever the flaws in the current constituency boundaries, it is at least pleasing to note just how many marginal seats are within striking distance of a Malmaison. Other hotel chains are available, but not all of them have comfortable rooms, free Wi-Fi, noon check-out (allowing a full morning's work), and will serve you a proper dinner at 10 p.m., thus avoiding an ugly Clarkson-style confrontation. Nor do they all offer the facility of a free bar voucher when you order breakfast on check-in, so cocktails need not appear on your bill. Despite these factors, no methodological proprieties were harmed in the making of this book.

And so began Operation Rolling Thunder. The reports that follow are the result. They are set out here as they were published at the time, as though a diary of the campaign, with the addition of a short paragraph outlining the events of the preceding week, as a reminder of the political news that was at the time gripping – or, more likely, failing to grip – the nation.

When they were first published, the parts of these reports that won the most attention were what those in the business call "projective techniques": exercises in which we asked people to imagine, for example, the leaders as animals or cartoon characters, or what they would do on a free Friday night. (The answers to some of these questions are collected at various points throughout the book. They are not labelled but it should not be difficult to tell which assortment of images represents each leader.) This might sound like a gimmick, but such questions reveal some quite nuanced assessments. The answers to the question "If each party were a house, what would it be like?", offered on the spur of the moment by floating voters in Wolverhampton and Cheadle six weeks before election day, amount to an acute commentary on the parties' brand strengths and weaknesses.

All the quotes are completely genuine, and some of them are very funny, whether or not they were intended to be. Indeed, one reader tweeted that Lord Ashcroft's team seemed to be having more fun than anyone else in politics (and so we were, right up until 10 p.m. on election night and the exit poll that ruined every pollster's evening). The unintentional comedy is not included to make our participants look daft. People miss things, get the wrong end of the stick, conflate scandals, muddle policies and reveal staggering misapprehensions (my favourite being the idea that if you are registered to vote but don't turn out, your vote goes to the party in power). They can also be capricious and contradictory. The man who, many years ago, introduced himself to the group by saying his hobbies were "foreign travel and the Stop Stansted Expansion campaign" could almost be a mascot for our times.

But none of this is to mock the voters. In fact, the small confusions and minor misunderstandings illustrate a deeper truth, which is how little the daily trivialities of politics really matter. As is amply demonstrated here, people might fail to distinguish between blue, red and yellow plans for promoting apprenticeships, or forget which leader has two kitchens, but they know what is really going on. One focus group could make you despair of democracy. A hundred of them would make you rejoice in it.

CROYDON AND DUDLEY
13 & 15 January: 16 weeks to go

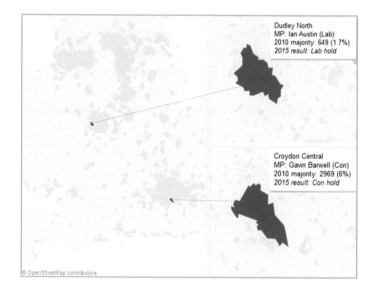

Dudley North
MP: Ian Austin (Lab)
2010 majority: 649 (1.7%)
2015 result: Lab hold

Croydon Central
MP: Gavin Barwell (Con)
2010 majority: 2969 (6%)
2015 result: Con hold

© OpenStreetMap contributors

The parties launched their New Year campaigns. David Cameron urged voters to "stay on the path to a stronger economy". Ed Miliband said Britain had become a country of "food banks and bank bonuses" and that the Tories would cut public spending back to the levels of the 1930s. The Lib Dems said they would link the amount of money going into public services to the growth of the economy. Cameron said he would not take part in TV election debates unless the Greens were represented. In Paris, two Islamist terrorists murdered twelve members of staff and one policeman in a raid on the offices of Charlie Hebdo, *a satirical magazine. A gunman and four hostages died in a subsequent siege at a supermarket.*

*

After all the frantic launching and speechmaking of the past fortnight, did the election feel imminent to our undecided voters in Croydon and Dudley? "I don't think there's been much in the media," observed a lady in a moment that would leave overworked party press officers with their heads in their hands. Others agreed: "There's no excitement building. It feels more like a local election. There's something coming but not anything big like who's going to run the country."

> *"There's no excitement building ... It feels like there's something coming but not anything big like who's going to run the country."*

One political story that most (but by no means all – "It's not the sort of thing that's on the local radio news") had spotted was the TV debate controversy. As Ed Miliband foresaw at last week's PMQs, "nobody but nobody" believed Cameron's objections to the proposed format were founded on a wish to be fair to the Greens: clearly he was "more worried about Farage" and wants someone "to take the heat off himself". Neither were they convinced that the Greens should be invited – they are, as one lady put it, "a bit more niche than UKIP".

But if Cameron's objections were transparently "a tactic", there was no outrage at his reluctance to take part, though all thought an empty prime ministerial chair amid the other leaders would look very bad indeed. Most said they would watch the debates if they were on (or at least the highlights – "I don't want to listen to an hour and a half of it"), but there was no indignation at the potential denial of anything they regarded as a democratic right. No. 10 is probably right to calculate that the PM has more to lose by taking part in debates than by being seen as the reason for their not happening at all.

Labour and the Conservatives launch their New Year campaigns

None of our participants had seen the rival posters launched by Labour and the Conservatives last week. What did they make of the Labour claim that "the Tories want to cut spending on public services back to the levels of the 1930s, when there was no NHS"?

"That seems very unlikely," frowned one fair-minded soul. "That's a lie. Nonsense. It's completely misleading," declared another. "That sort of thing annoys me," added another, and all agreed that "anything like that you take with a pinch of salt". The trouble is, "There are cuts behind the scenes and there is sneaking privatisation." Therefore, "there is a grain of truth, or more than a grain" in Labour's claim, extreme exaggeration though it is.

The Conservative poster urging voters to "stay on the road to a stronger economy" was better received. People thought the message was positive, powerful and largely believable, although they questioned some of the specifics.

There was also a lesson in the ambiguities of the verbless political sentence. "1.75 million more people in work. 760,000 more businesses. The deficit halved" proclaims the poster. "Are they predictions?" someone asked. Most realised they were things the government had achieved, or at least claims to have done. Again, though, the figures could not be taken at face value: "They will be at the minimum wage, most of those jobs, or zero-hour contracts." Still, the message of the poster chimed with most people's view that the economy was improving overall – if not yet for them personally – and was, at any rate, "better than a cheap snipe".

*

Over the next four months, people will be bombarded with facts and statistics, not least from the parties. How will people make sense of them? Any such "fact" that comes from a party will be immediately discounted as being misleading or incomplete, even if it may contain a kernel of truth. Analysis from the BBC could not be regarded as gospel, since reporters could have biases of their own and even they had to get their figures from somewhere.

Official statistics from sources like the Office for Budget Responsibility were only so much help, since different parties and commentators would interpret them in different ways. Even think tanks like the Institute for Fiscal Studies could not be taken entirely at face value: "Are they totally independent? You don't always know if the government is behind them or where they get their funding." When it comes down to it, "You just have to read as much as possible and come to your own view."

"When you're not going to win, you can say whatever you like, like Clegg used to."

How were the party leaders coming across at this stage of the game? As always, people observed that Nigel Farage was a bit different from other leaders and less stuffy, but there was more than a note of scepticism – particularly in Croydon, and particularly among participants from ethnic minorities. "You get where he's coming from, but it's the way he says it – like the Romanians moving in next door and people not speaking English on the train." He also has the luxury that "when you're not going to win, you can say whatever you like, like Clegg used to".

A number of people noted that they had only heard UKIP talk about Europe and (especially) immigration – a complaint that had not surfaced for some time in our research but which may be more of a problem for the party as the election approaches. For that reason, some were keen to hear what he would have to say in the TV debates, should they happen – a platform that could give him the chance to defy expectations by broadening some people's view of UKIP, which confirms the wisdom of Downing Street's reluctance to take part.

As is often the case, comments about Nick Clegg were not so much critical as sympathetic, which does not augur well for May ("He's trying his best … he was always on a hiding to nothing").

In the wake of the Paris attacks, people's remarks about David Cameron often focused on the need for strong leadership in an uncertain world – a role that, from the candidates on offer, they could only imagine him fulfilling: "You need someone in authority who looks like they can cope with it."

"Miliband feels like the interim Labour leader,
until the next one."

Perhaps the most notable feature of these groups of undecided voters was the absence of any enthusiasm for Labour – even among those who had voted for the party in 2010 – or any urgent desire for change. Nobody could recall any Labour promises, and the most positive thing anyone said about Ed Miliband was that "he talks sense on things like not privatising the NHS, but he's not really on the ball, not in David Cameron's league". People could not say where he wanted to take Britain: "He hasn't really made up his mind where he's going … it's as though he just wants to be a politician, and he's faffing around to find some principles" – and, ominously, "It feels like he's the interim Labour leader, until the next one."

"Clegg is like a Chihuahua in David
Cameron's handbag."

If each leader were an animal, what would they be? Cameron would be a fox, being smart and sleek – or, less charitably, "a giraffe, looking down on everybody". Farage? A peacock, or a weasel. Clegg? "A Chihuahua in David Cameron's handbag." Miliband? Puzzlement. "Certainly not a predator … one of those animals that, when you go to the zoo, you're not bothered whether you see it or not."

BRIGHTON AND SOLIHULL
20 & 22 January: 15 weeks to go

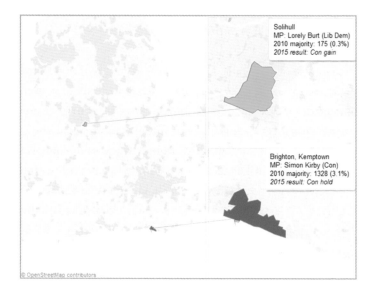

Solihull
MP: Lorely Burt (Lib Dem)
2010 majority: 175 (0.3%)
2015 result: Con gain

Brighton, Kemptown
MP: Simon Kirby (Con)
2010 majority: 1328 (3.1%)
2015 result: Con hold

© OpenStreetMap contributors

Broadcasters published revised election debate proposals, which included two seven-way events involving the Conservatives, Labour, the Liberal Democrats, UKIP, the Green Party, Plaid Cymru and the Scottish National Party; the Conservatives said the plan "would be considered as part of the ongoing debates process". David Cameron accused Ed Miliband of using the NHS as a "political weapon". The government published a draft bill to transfer more powers to the Scottish Parliament. The oil price fell below $50 a barrel, a decline of more than 60 per cent since the previous June. The World Economic Forum met in Davos.

*

Our latest round of focus groups, conducted last week in Brighton and Solihull, confirmed that undecided voters had detected the first signs of easing on the cost of living. However, this could not be credited to the government: "It's not that the economy is better, it's that we're not paying out as much for food and petrol" – they had "Aldi versus Lidl" and "the Arabs flooding the world with oil" to thank.

In general, there was more optimism than pessimism about prospects for the economy, but most did not yet think the recovery had got as far as them: "They tell us it's better, but how many have had a pay rise in the last three or four years?"

Nor did people expect any dramatic improvement – continued austerity, probably under any government, would mean things continuing on the same path for the next few years. Some wondered how long they would have to wait to feel the benefits. As one lady said when told the Tories talked about their long-term economic plan, "Yes, but *how* long?"

*

Only a few recalled Labour's proposed energy-price freeze, but with that policy obsolete, little else from the party had broken through. Some observed that they had been "banging on about the NHS", but to what end they were not sure. Most saw it as a stick with which Labour intended to beat the Tories; nobody had heard of any Labour plan to improve the service, other than possibly to spend more: "They're saying what's wrong with it, not what they're going to do to put it right"; "They care about it deep down and they would try to do more, but they're a bit stupid with the money."

"Labour care about the NHS deep down and they
would try to do more, but they're a bit stupid with the money."

There was a widespread view that problems with the NHS were deep-seated, did not originate with the current government and would not be solved by the next one: "The problems are on the ground. It's not really something that can be solved in parliament. It will take years."

The only other message that had so far got through from Labour was the proposed Mansion Tax, which received a decidedly mixed response, usually because it would unfairly punish people of modest means who had lived all their lives in the same home: "There are people like my wife's grandmother, who has lived in the same house in Surrey since 1922. She's not a rich woman." As dangerous for Labour politically was a suspicion that the policy was motivated mainly by envy and dislike of success: "It rallies people who are irritated that 'everyone else is doing better than me'"; "When they talk about taxing the rich, they're scapegoating. In the same way UKIP say 'it's the foreigners', Labour say 'it's rich people'."

Little had got through from the Conservatives either, other than a general message about staying on the path of austerity and restoring stability. None could recall any of the Tories' six election themes, though a few had heard that the NHS was not among them.

*

Those who had voted Liberal Democrat in 2010 other than as a left-wing alternative to Labour were notably open to Nick Clegg's pitch that neither Labour nor the Conservatives could be trusted to govern alone. The Lib Dems had acted as the

Tories' "conscience" and had tempered their excesses: "When you think of what austerity could have been like without the Lib Dems..." With the Conservatives still in need of toning down and Labour failing to inspire confidence, this remained a good argument for sticking with the Lib Dems – particularly since UKIP would hardly be a moderating influence ("They said they wanted to ban breastfeeding in public!").

*

In Brighton, most of those who had voted for the Green MP Caroline Lucas in 2010 thought highly of her and were inclined to support her again. This was despite their almost unanimous disdain for the Green-run local council, which they said had allowed rubbish to pile up in the streets and brought traffic to a state of semi-permanent gridlock. Others, who were unlikely to have considered the Greens in the first place, marvelled at what they had heard of the party's policies ("They want to legalise membership of Al-Qaeda and give everyone £70 a week!").

*

It is not surprising that most participants had heard little from the parties given that the only political story that had made any impression on them was about process. The TV debate saga was always the first thing to be mentioned spontaneously, and the proposed 7–7–2 format was announced hours before our Solihull groups. As noted last week, whether the debates go ahead or not is unlikely to shift many votes itself, but our group were keen to watch them if they happened and liked the idea of a wider field: "People want to hear what the newbies have to say." The problem was that with such a wide field, "it will either go on forever or we won't get to hear much from each of them if there are seven answers to each question".

*

Finally, to reveal more of the psychology of voters' underlying perceptions, the crucial question of the week: if each party leader were a car, what car would they be?

There was a surprising consensus in both venues about Nick Clegg: he would be a Smart car, unless he was a people carrier to cart round all the baggage. Ed Miliband was more difficult: "A Ford Focus; average. Actually, no, a Ford Focus is reliable." David Cameron would be "something smooth", possibly a Mercedes or a Range Rover, "depending on the image he wanted that day". On Nigel Farage, the groups were divided: a Ford Capri ("tinted windows, pimped"), with a "shiny exterior but then you look under the bonnet"; or "a four-by-four with illegal bull bars on the front. Or a tank."

SUTTON AND ELMET
27 & 29 January: 14 weeks to go

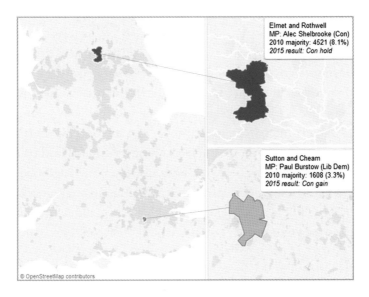

Elmet and Rothwell
MP: Alec Shelbrooke (Con)
2010 majority: 4521 (8.1%)
2015 result: Con hold

Sutton and Cheam
MP: Paul Burstow (Lib Dem)
2010 majority: 1608 (3.3%)
2015 result: Con gain

© OpenStreetMap contributors

The left-wing populist party Syriza was elected in Greece on a promise to end austerity. With 100 days to go until the election, the Liberal Democrats launched a poster to highlight their aim of preventing the other parties "lurching to the extremes of left and right". A Conservative poster depicted Ed Miliband arm in arm with Alex Salmond under the headline: "Your worst nightmare … just got worse." David Cameron set out plans to cut the benefits cap from £26,000 to £23,000 per year. Labour pledged 5,000 new home care workers, 8,000 new GPs and 20,000 new nurses in the NHS.

*

Judging by this week's focus groups in Sutton & Cheam and

Elmet & Rothwell, people are at least starting to notice that the election will soon be upon them. Even so, the process story of the TV debates continues to be heard above any matters of substance. For most people, it was clear that David Cameron was trying to avoid taking part.

"Cameron is starting to look like a debate dodger."

While his reasons were understandable as far as his own interests were concerned ("It's because he struggles with the UKIP leader. But don't we all?"), he was starting to look to some like a "debate dodger" who ought to be more willing to submit himself to questioning "out his comfort zone". Notably, though, those who were already the most hostile to the PM argued this point the most strongly. Downing Street evidently judges, probably rightly, that this impression will ultimately be less damaging than taking part in the debates on the wrong terms.

*

Events in Greece have few parallels with Britain, as far as our participants were concerned. In fact, it was not clear to everyone quite what those events had been: "It was something to do with the economy not doing very well." Most felt the situation there did not apply here in the same way or to the same extent, having arisen essentially from "the Greeks being Greeks", not paying their taxes and expecting the EU to bail them out from the consequences of their profligacy. As a result, they had been through "hell, riots, anarchy". If there is a moral to the story it is "don't borrow too much" and "don't listen to fake promises". And, for some, it was one more reason to prefer stability at home in an uncertain world, rather than evidence that austerity could be ended by voting against it.

*

One message that had begun to percolate through to people was Labour's focus on the NHS, though apart from a promise to protect rather than "privatise" the service, few had noted the details of "how many more nurses we're going to get, and all that malarkey". The specifics of Labour's pledge – including 5,000 new home care workers, 8,000 new GPs, and 20,000 new nurses – seemed to our groups to amount almost to a caricature of a suspect political promise. It sounded completely unrealistic ("Where is he going to get 8,000 GPs?") and unaffordable ("How expensive is that? The biggest problem we've got is balancing the books"; "Is it the Mansion Tax? It's going to save the world, that."). And while the new staff would be welcome if they ever materialised, the policy did not sound like an attempt to deal with the deeper problems facing the NHS. The risk to Labour is that an approach designed to highlight one of the party's strengths will have the effect of reinforcing perhaps its biggest weakness. As one floating voter put it: "Labour are theoretically better on the NHS because they spend, but the money they spend is borrowed."

"Where is Miliband going to get 8,000 GPs?"

David Cameron's promise to reduce the benefit cap, by contrast, was thought to be both practical and right. Some observed that £23,000 went a lot further in some parts of the country than others, but the principle – "You shouldn't be able to earn more not working than you do working" – was supported overwhelmingly. "It's a great idea. A lot of people who work with me are skilled and have degrees and are only on about twenty-two." A few also said they had heard Cameron talking about ensuring new immigrants could not claim benefits immediately – to which their only objection was to wonder why they had been allowed to do so up till now.

The Liberal Democrats pledge to prevent the Tories and Labour "lurching to the extremes"

In Sutton, where our constituency polls suggest the Lib Dems are so far defying the national tide, local issues and Paul Burstow's reputation had played a big part in people's 2010 voting decisions and seemed set to do so again. Nationally, the party's own road poster, steering between reckless borrowing to the left and reckless cuts to the right, summed up the Lib Dems' approach for these participants – for whom staying the course, as urged by the Tories, meant voting as they did last time. But those who did not vote Lib Dem in 2010, or did so in West Yorkshire, were either dissatisfied with this rather non-specific approach or did not accept that the party was still equidistant between Labour and the Tories: "I struggle with the whole Lib Dem thing since the coalition – he might as well be a Tory."

*

The Conservative poster featuring Ed Miliband and Alex Salmond outside No. 10 beneath the legend "Your worst nightmare … just got worse" caused some amusement. People disliked the idea of a Labour–SNP government ("a recipe for disaster"), which reflects the finding of our poll last year that found a majority, including most Labour voters, saying they would be unhappy with the SNP being part of a coalition at Westminster.

The Conservatives raise the prospect of a Labour government dependent on the SNP

But the main effect of the poster in the groups was not to warn of the dangers of Labour, but to stoke resentment of the SNP and what they saw as Scotland's unreasonable demands for preferential treatment. "The amount of time and effort they've all gone to because they're so desperate to get their additional powers. Why is Scotland so bloody special? Their kids get university for free, they get free prescriptions, and they're still moaning." We will see as the campaign unfolds whether the Scottish factor comes to play a part in English voters' decisions.

"Why is Scotland so bloody special? Their kids get university for free, they get free prescriptions, and they're still moaning."

At the end of the first month of the election year, what do the parties' campaigns boil down to? The Greens have yet to break through everywhere, though in a world where few can name any parties' policies, their proposal to legalise membership of terrorist organisations has achieved impressive cut-through. But, for these voters, their message in a nutshell remained "Vote Green to save the planet".

UKIP's message was "Leave the EU and control immigration" (with some adding "smoke in pubs again"). But the other recurring theme for the party, also noted last week, was that they were a "one-trick pony": "What else have they got? If they were in government, what would they do about the NHS?"

Other than in Sutton, where people heard the Lib Dems' message as "Save St Helier Hospital", no such specific ideas attached themselves to the party. It amounted to "Vote Lib Dem to balance the extremes – to split the difference".

Ed Miliband's message so far – not entirely convincing, for the reasons described above – was simply "Vote Labour to save the NHS". Some added "… and stop the cuts" or "… and tax the rich".

The Conservatives would have been pleased to hear their message described as "Finish the job and get back on track", though not everyone was sure the economy was really on the right course. Accordingly, few were yet certain about where their cross would end up. "If [the messages] were anonymous, I'd like the Labour one, but now I struggle. The Tories haven't sorted the economy out but I just can't see myself voting for Ed Miliband." Some said they would probably decide on the way to the polling station.

> *"The Tories haven't sorted the economy out,*
> *but I just can't see myself voting for Ed Miliband."*

Finally, thanks to all the Twitter followers who suggested questions to reveal more about voters' perceptions. We will use as many as we can, but this week (with thanks to Chris Deerin) ... party leaders as cartoon characters. Mr Cameron? "Top Cat. He doesn't get flustered," or, for those who took a less benign view, Dick Dastardly. Mr Clegg? The clean-cut but somewhat ineffectual Fred Jones from *Scooby-Doo*. Mr Miliband? The hapless but by no means unlikeable Deputy Dawg, or possibly Elmer Fudd, in perennial but fruitless pursuit of the prime ministerial wabbit. For Mr Farage we have another example of what the *Telegraph*'s Stephen Bush has called the Sean Bean/Mr Bean dichotomy: is the real UKIP leader Andy Capp or Cruella de Vil?

RAMSGATE AND BURY
3 & 5 February: 13 weeks to go

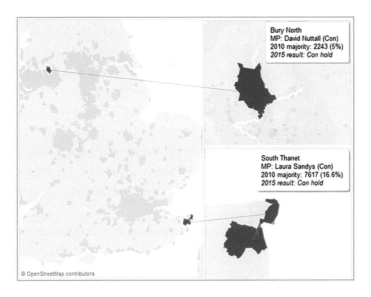

Bury North
MP: David Nuttall (Con)
2010 majority: 2243 (5%)
2015 result: Con hold

South Thanet
MP: Laura Sandys (Con)
2010 majority: 7617 (16.6%)
2015 result: Con hold

© OpenStreetMap contributors

William Hague set out Conservative plans for "English votes for English laws", under which Scottish MPs at Westminster would be prevented from voting on measures on policy areas that were devolved to Holyrood. Stefano Pessina, the acting chief executive of Boots, said a Labour government under Ed Miliband would be a "catastrophe" for Britain, as the party's policies were "not helpful for business". Labour claimed Mr Pessina was a "tax exile" who lived in Monaco.

*

The qualities of the Prime Minister and his opposite number were a critical factor for many of last week's undecided focus-group participants in Ramsgate and Bury. It has long been clear that the result in May will largely hang on how people resolve their dilemma when they prefer Labour to the Tories, but Cameron to Miliband. Several people in our groups, including some who voted Labour in 2010, said the Labour leader was the single biggest barrier to their taking the party seriously. Though some felt he was "genuine" and "really does care", the downside was that he "couldn't lead a procession" and "doesn't seem to have confidence in his own beliefs".

Cameron, who for some had a lack of empathy with less well-off people that led him to make mistakes, was nevertheless "decisive" and "exudes confidence", which were crucial attributes in uncertain times: "You've got to have a Prime Minister who looks the part when he represents the country and I think he does that."

Among the hefty proportion of voters who think it makes little difference who wins, but do not want to spend their vote on one of what they see as the protest parties, some will revert to the party that they think best shares their values. But a proportion will look at it differently: for them, if the result is neither here nor there, we might as well have someone who knows what he's about. "Cameron is cutting council budgets, but is Miliband going to do anything different? So you might as well go for someone who gives you confidence."

"You've got to have a Prime Minister who looks the part when he represents the country and I think Cameron does that."

The Labour *v.* Boots row, which around half our participants recalled when reminded (people generally admit it when something has passed them by), appears to have ended in a score draw. Stefano Pessina, the company's chief executive, warned last week that Labour's policies would be a "catastrophe" for business. But Labour's attack on Mr Pessina's tax status had gone some way to neutralising the effect of his words. As a major employer, Mr Pessina "probably has his finger on the pulse somewhere", and for some it was "a bit of a concern if this is the best response Labour can come up with. It's not really answering the point he made." But for others, their indignation over the tax question invalidated his other points, and some went as far as to say it had done more to put them off Boots than Labour.

*

The idea of "English votes for English laws" had not managed to capture the imagination of our participants, or sometimes their understanding ("Is it when you've got to prove you're English for certain things, like using the NHS?"). Most people supported the idea that laws only affecting England should ultimately be decided only by MPs representing England, though some thought such laws might be difficult to distinguish. However, nobody claimed the issue would affect their vote: "It's not the biggest deal of the day."

What it did do, like the Miliband–Salmond poster discussed in last week's groups, was highlight division and remind people of SNP demands for extra powers, despite what people regarded as Scotland's already favourable arrangements on things like tuition fees and prescription charges. "Every time Nicola Sturgeon comes on the telly you just get the feeling she *hates* us. She's so angry." As one participant lamented, "We used to be quite unified but now it's all splinter groups."

*

As previous groups had noticed, Ed Miliband seems always to be "on about the National Health Service", though Labour's attempts to blame problems in the NHS on the Conservatives were not altogether convincing. "A lot of people are going to A&E for sore thumbs," and, after all, whoever is in government, "it's still managed by the same managers". As for privatisation – which people loosely define as anybody making a profit at any stage, or any kind of outsourcing, or charging, or anything else that sounds remotely disagreeable (only a few took the view that "if it's reducing the waiting list and you get the same service, it doesn't matter") – the coalition had not introduced the idea: "Labour did it with the buildings and the Tories carried it on."

*

In Ramsgate, part of the South Thanet constituency, most did not much mind that Nigel Farage had chosen the place to stand for parliament because of the chance it gave him of being elected. Most of those inclined to consider UKIP said they would either have voted for the party whoever was standing or liked the idea of being represented by such a prominent figure, not least because they felt the area had seen better days and needed a boost: "There's no port any more, no airport – there are two industries here: shop work and care." None of our small sample of participants was very excited about Al Murray's Pub Landlord candidacy: "He's a piss-taker. The same as the Monster Raving Loonies."

"Every time you see Farage he has a glass in his hand. You think, 'Well, you're going to save the nation, aren't you?'"

More widely, most of those who did not support UKIP were nonetheless glad they were there. Though they did not always take Farage very seriously ("Every time you see him he has a glass in his hand. You think, 'Well, you're going to save the nation, aren't you?'"), they thought he was performing a useful service in creating debate about issues other parties would rather ignore. Some even rather admired him: "If you look at what he's done, four or five years ago you wouldn't have believed it."

But even some of his admirers and potential voters accepted that Farage was able to make declarations and promises secure in the knowledge that he would never have to deliver on them. This is why the other parties find the UKIP phenomenon so frustrating. They want to tell the voters to grow up and pull themselves together – unlikely to be a winning message.

*

At this stage, what were people's biggest reservations when it came to each party? For the Greens and UKIP, it was the fear of wasting a vote in the greater scheme of things, even though UKIP were in contention in one of the seats: "They're both about posing the idea rather than getting into government." For UKIP, people also mentioned "policies they don't voice, like cutting maternity leave" and, in both destinations, a suspicion that the party might harbour unsavoury factions.

The biggest doubt about the Lib Dems was simply that "you get the feeling they're finished", and that they had "lost their soul" after the experience of coalition – though they were not a big factor in either of the seats we visited this week.

The two main reservations about Labour were that "they would go back to how they were before – spend, spend, spend", and Ed Miliband himself – "He just waffles … he stops me getting into Labour."

For the Conservatives, it was the traditional fear that "they're more interested in the shareholders than the workers", and their inability to keep their promise on immigration cast doubt on future pledges.

What, then, did people make of the Tory mantra of "chaos versus competence"? Neither quite hit the mark, though the Conservatives had the better claim to competence than their rivals. But "chaos" was not quite the fear generated by Labour. Most struggled to come up with such a pithy description of their own, but, for some, a theme was beginning to emerge: "The entire battle is about long-term solutions versus short-term solutions and throwing money at things."

"The entire battle is about long-term solutions versus short-term solutions and throwing money at things."

Finally, the question on the lips of most serious commentators: if each leader were a beverage, what beverage would they be? Mr Farage, predictably enough, would be the pint of bitter that is his trademark. The PM? A good red wine ("full bodied, decent percentage"), a G&T or James Bond's Vesper martini. Mr Clegg would be a Babycham, or perhaps a Woo Woo, which, as aficionados will know, is a cocktail comprising vodka, peach schnapps and cranberry, not simply a belief in the irrational or unfounded. Mr Miliband? Crème de menthe, "the sort of drink nobody would order". Or a non-alcoholic beer. "Or a Bloody Mary. Actually, no, just a tomato juice."

LOUGHBOROUGH AND SHEFFIELD
10 & 12 February: 12 weeks to go

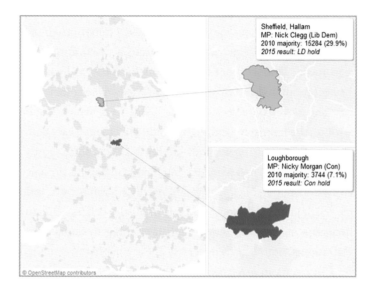

Sheffield, Hallam
MP: Nick Clegg (Lib Dem)
2010 majority: 15284 (29.9%)
2015 result: LD hold

Loughborough
MP: Nicky Morgan (Con)
2010 majority: 3744 (7.1%)
2015 result: Con hold

© OpenStreetMap contributors

Harriet Harman launched Labour's "Woman to Woman" minibus, part of the party's campaign aimed at female voters; debate ensued as to whether or not the bus was pink. George Osborne announced the extension of Pensioner Bonds, which offered competitive interest rates for savers aged over sixty-five. David Cameron called on firms to give workers a pay rise. Ed Miliband said a Labour government would double paid paternity leave for new fathers to four weeks. The PM was criticised for having appointed Lord Green, the former chairman of HSBC, as a trade minister, after the bank's Swiss arm was accused of helping customers avoid tax.

*

This week's focus groups with undecided voters took place in Loughborough and Sheffield Hallam. The identity of the sitting MPs was well known in both places, but it was not clear that a high national profile would necessarily be an advantage to either.

Nicky Morgan, the Education Secretary and Conservative MP for Loughborough, was regarded as an assiduous local campaigner but some worried that her promotion to the Cabinet may have been a distraction from her first duty: "You get someone who says they will stand up for the local area, then they get promoted and they're not interested." One complained that "she moved here because it was a safe seat", which will be news to the minister who, as a candidate, spent years campaigning in a constituency that Labour had held since 1997.

The Deputy Prime Minister also clearly makes his presence felt in Sheffield. ("Nick Clegg sent me a Christmas card," said one participant. "Me too!" chimed in all the others.) But the discussion showed just how tough it is going to be to please disillusioned 2010 Lib Dem voters. These constituents credited the Lib Dems in government with the Pupil Premium, free school meals and the raising of the income tax threshold, as well as being a moderating influence on the Tories – all of which they praised, and all of which Clegg would claim as major Lib Dem achievements. But many could still not excuse the deal with the Conservatives, or the reversal on tuition fees: "He traded that for a ministerial car." The argument that a junior coalition party inevitably has to take what it can get (and had indeed scored a number of successes that they themselves welcomed) was not enough for them because the promise to vote against the fee rise had been so public and unequivocal. What would he let them down on next time? The DPM has a fight on his hands.

"Why is she going round in a pink van?"

Labour's "Woman to Woman" campaign bus

The women of Sheffield did not feel patronised by the hue of Harriet Harman's campaign bus so much as bemused: "Why is she going round in a pink van?" They were also doubtful about its purpose ("Is there a blue bus saying these are the issues for men, let's go and talk to the men?") and the slogan, which seemed more suited to a specialist dating agency ("'Woman to Woman?' That sounds like, er, something else"). Still, as one lady observed, "It's done its job, it's on the national news." Is that the view at Labour HQ?

*

Our participants had found nothing about the row over HSBC and tax very enlightening or surprising. Though they questioned whether Lord Green should have been appointed a minister, nobody thought it much of a revelation that such a thing might have occurred: "You just expect that's what's happening." For some, though, it did underline what they saw as double standards on the part of the Conservatives: "They're focusing on benefit cheats, which is a very Tory thing to do, talking about slackers, compared to people who don't pay the taxes they owe – they just slap them on the wrist and say, 'Would you like to pay it back?'"

The groups in both constituencies had noted the pledge to extend Pensioner Bonds. Most participants were not pensioners and were not impressed. "Cameron has offered something to the oldies. It's a bribe, a vote-grabber" – though nothing was very surprising about this either: "They do that with loads and loads of things." On the upside for the PM, some thought the pledge had been made by Labour.

> *"Cameron has offered something to the oldies.*
> *It's a bribe, a vote-grabber."*

Labour's pledge to double paternity leave had also caught our participants' attention – though in our groups, the women were rather more impressed than the men. The mothers usually liked the idea of extra family time, with several noting that arrangements in Europe seem more civilised in this regard. But for some of the men: "It's another one of those promises that gets the headline, but when you look at the detail it's barely the minimum wage. What is it, £260 a week? People can't afford to take it. I couldn't." There were also practical considerations, especially for small businesses: "If you employ people it looks a bit different. The government pay for it, but it's the absence, the workload it creates for everyone else."

*

For those warily considering the options, what questions did each party have to answer to seal the deal? The Greens, as we have heard before, need to convince people that their vote would not be wasted when issues outside the party's usual realm of interest are at stake: "People are more concerned with making ends meet, jobs, the NHS, the ageing population – so what can the Green Party bring to the table?" People were also concerned about the implications of their proposals for the cost of living: "Going green, with lightbulbs and things, is *always* more expensive. How much is it going to cost?" Some had also detected what they regarded as a rather authoritarian approach: "They want to make things nice for the community and nice for the sky, but if you don't want it, you're having it."

With UKIP, along with doubts about their approach to issues other than Europe and immigration, there were concerns that "extreme" views lurked below the surface and some wondered about "the hierarchy behind Farage". Intriguingly, some also felt there would be "a bit of a social stigma" surrounding the party: "For me it would be, 'What would people say if they found out?' People judge you on it. They say they don't, but they do." Others who were not considering UKIP corroborated this: "If someone told me they were voting UKIP, I'd think differently about them. I'd be surprised they'd been sucked in." This was as much about what they saw as the futility of such a vote as any disapproval of the party's policies or rhetoric: "I couldn't understand it. I would always vote for people who can change things and get into government and achieve something."

"I didn't know what to do last time, I was very confused, so I voted Liberal Democrat."

For the Lib Dems, as reflected in the earlier discussion on the merits of Mr Clegg, the question in the minds of many was how robustly the party would stick to its pre-election positions if it found itself back in coalition negotiations: "Are they going to roll over again like last time?" Some also wondered how, as one put it, they would achieve a "conscious uncoupling" from the Conservatives. (Certainly they will no longer be able to rely on the votes of people like the lady who quite literally said: "I didn't know what to do last time, I was very confused, so I voted Liberal Democrat.")

Doubtful potential Labour voters wondered "whether they can be trusted with the economy", or, to put it another way, "Where will they get the money from?" The party's reluctance to face up to what they regarded as its responsibilities when last in office was an important factor: "Acknowledge what happened, that you were in power for a long time and some negative things happened. Own it. Don't just say it's all gone wrong in the last four and a half years." Some who were naturally sympathetic to the party were also waiting for a compelling reason to vote for it: "There seems to be no vision or real belief, nothing that gets me excited about Labour"; "If the Tories get in again, it will be because there was no real alternative."

> *"I work in the public sector, so I'm worried that*
> *if they get back in, they really* **will** *finish the job."*

For these participants, questions about the Conservatives concerned austerity. First, how far would they go when it came to public sector cuts, and were their tax credits safe? "I work in the public sector, so I'm worried that if they get back in, they really *will* finish the job." Second, how long would it last and what did they have to look forward to at the end of it? "I just want to be out of the pit. It's been going on for years. When *are* we going to be out of it?" "The job is half done at the moment.

It's part one. But if they haven't done it by the end of part two there isn't going to be a part three."

*

It being Oscars week, we need to know who the nation thinks should play the part of each leader in the movie of his life. Our participants struggled somewhat with Mr Clegg, though he will not be too dismayed with the suggestion of Tom Cruise or Kevin Bacon. There was a wide consensus that Hugh Grant or Colin Firth should be cast as David Cameron, though whether either would be happy to play him is another question. There was even wider agreement – and it must be emphasised that all these suggestions are unprompted – that Mr Miliband would be best portrayed by Rowan Atkinson, in character as Mr Bean. As so often, a division over the image of Mr Farage: for some, he is Ray Winstone; for others, Sid James.

HALESOWEN AND TAUNTON
17 & 19 February: 11 weeks to go

Halesowen and Rowley Regis
MP: James Morris (Con)
2010 majority: 2023 (4.6%)
2015 result: Con hold

Taunton Deane
MP: Jeremy Browne (Lib Dem)
2010 majority: 3993 (6.9%)
2015 result: Con gain

© OpenStreetMap contributors

Labour launched its economic plan aimed at achieving "inclusive prosperity"; it included 80,000 new apprenticeships, an £8 per hour minimum wage by 2020, "everyday workers" on companies' remuneration committees, and the lowest Corporation Tax in the G7. David Cameron said it was not fair that taxpayers should have to fund sickness benefits for people with treatable conditions who refused to seek help. He also proposed that 18–21-year-olds should spend thirty hours a week doing voluntary work and ten hours looking for a job in order to qualify for benefits. Ed Balls said people should ask for receipts for cash-in-hand jobs like hedge cutting. A survey suggested three-quarters of FTSE500 bosses thought a Conservative government would be best for their business. It was revealed that Tory donors were among those with accounts in Switzerland with HSBC's private bank.

*

This week's focus groups with undecided voters were held in Halesowen and Taunton, where the parties' local campaigns had begun to swing into action. Leaflets and direct mail had begun to arrive, not all of it very enlightening: "The Labour one said if you vote Tory the NHS will be privatised and the Tory one said if you vote Labour spending will be out of control." There was also a lesson in proofreading: "I got a letter from the Lib Dems but there was a terrible typo in the main headline so I didn't look at the rest of it."

In Taunton, most participants knew the Lib Dem incumbent Jeremy Browne was standing down ("He fell out with Nick Clegg. He was Under-Foreign Secretary or something and got the sack"). He was visible and well known locally, though there was some dispute as to whether this meant he was a good MP or merely "likes having his photo taken".

The Conservative challenger Rebecca Pow was also mentioned by name by several people in the groups – a rare feat for a candidate. Even so, most of those who had voted Lib Dem last time said they would probably do so again, either because they thought the party had done reasonably well in office on things like the tax threshold and free school meals, or because they were simply the local alternative to the Conservatives.

"I got a letter from the Lib Dems but there was a terrible typo in the main headline so I didn't look at the rest of it."

In national news, people in all the groups had noticed the Conservative plan to require young claimants to do voluntary work in return for benefits. People largely approved of this plan, both because it would be good for the young people concerned – "They need something instead of going into that rut where they are on benefits and have no idea what working is like" – and in terms of fairness to the taxpayer ("There's a hotline where you can dob people in," we were reminded with relish in Halesowen, where two participants had used this service to report neighbours they suspected of claiming more than their due).

People had also heard, and most supported in principle, the idea that people claiming benefits because of drug addiction or obesity should have to accept help for those problems. However, many thought there would be practical problems enforcing the policy and that it sounded rather a blunt instrument, particularly when it came to obesity. Some doubted the plan would ever be implemented: "They're not going to take their benefits away though, are they? Then they would be on the streets, and that's not going to happen."

*

The plan to expand apprenticeships had also been noticed, though not everyone was sure whose plan it was: "I can't remember what party it is, but someone has been promising apprenticeships for people with the right grades. I think it was the Lib Dems." The idea was welcomed, but those who did know it had originated from Labour wondered how much it would cost and how it would be paid for – something our groups this year have done in respect of all the Labour proposals that have crossed their radar. A few wondered what was in it for them: "We are always hearing about helping the kids, but what about people who have been working for twenty or thirty years? They just put your tax up." The proposal to raise the minimum wage to £8 an hour by 2020 generated little excitement: "By then it will only be worth what it is now".

"There are so many ways of dodging tax – invest in a film, buy a forest – it's been going on for decades. Did Labour really change anything in the thirteen years they were in government?"

For our groups, the ongoing rows about HSBC, tax avoidance and political donors had melded into a single shapeless story ("There was the guy with the Swiss bank account who hadn't paid tax for twenty years but they didn't prosecute. Wasn't it the Boots man?").

They had not found any of it very edifying, but neither was it very surprising, and our participants did not think of it as a party-political question, let alone a decisive election issue: "There are so many ways of dodging tax – invest in a film, buy a forest – it's been going on for decades. You go to your accountant and say, 'I don't want to pay any tax,' and he'll come back and say, 'OK, invest in this and this.' Did Labour really change it in the thirteen years they were in government?"

The news that a survey had revealed 77 per cent of FTSE500 business leaders thought a Conservative government would be the best outcome for their business was also far from conclusive: "They probably just think *they* would be better off under the Tories."

"Farage is a bit like your missus. He might have said something intelligent but you weren't really paying attention."

Views of the party leaders are now entrenched and are unlikely to change before polling day. As ever, the main question over David Cameron – usually raised by people more hostile to the Conservatives to start with – was whether he related to people from humbler origins than himself (the more open-minded saying, "As long as he's taking the right decisions for Britain, I'm not bothered about his background"); more often he was praised for standing up for the country, making difficult decisions or at least being "the best we've got".

Ed Miliband was, for some, a barrier to taking Labour seriously, and was not a strong leader despite having a steely side, if not a very attractive one: "He has got balls because he stabbed his own brother in public. That was absolutely ruthless, I wouldn't have done it."

Nick Clegg's attempts to make his voice heard in the coalition inspired more sympathy than admiration, and Nigel Farage was generally thought an invigorating person to have around even by those who would not consider voting UKIP (though some who regarded the party's agenda as being too narrow treated him as a sideshow: "He's a bit like your missus. He might have said something intelligent but you weren't really paying attention.").

> *"Ed Miliband would go to Waitrose, but with his Lidl bag-for-life to carry round afterwards."*

But what, you are asking, if each of the leaders were a supermarket? For our groups, the answer to this important question was that Nigel Farage would be Aldi: "You know what you're getting. Down to earth. Anyone can shop there." Nick Clegg would be the Co-op, with "all its nice fair-trade values" (if this sounds like a compliment, the tone of voice suggested it was not intended as one). David Cameron would inevitably be Waitrose, but "pretending to be Sainsbury's". Ed Miliband, by the same token, would "go to Waitrose but with his Lidl bag-for-life to carry round afterwards".

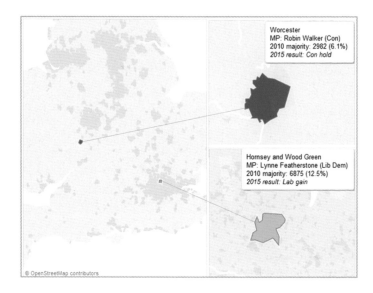

Worcester
MP: Robin Walker (Con)
2010 majority: 2982 (6.1%)
2015 result: Con hold

Hornsey and Wood Green
MP: Lynne Featherstone (Lib Dem)
2010 majority: 6875 (12.5%)
2015 result: Lab gain

© OpenStreetMap contributors

Jack Straw and Sir Malcolm Rifkind were caught out in a sting operation conducted by the Daily Telegraph *and the Channel 4* Dispatches *programme in which they were filmed offering their services to a fictitious Chinese company for payment. Green leader Natalie Bennett gave an interview on* LBC *in which she apparently forgot the details of her party's housing policy: "I had a brain fade, that happens," she later explained. David Cameron announced that a Conservative government would keep the Winter Fuel Allowance, free* TV *licences and bus passes for all pensioners. Ed Miliband pledged to reduce the cap on university tuition fees from £9,000 to £6,000 per year. A councillor, Rozanne Duncan, was expelled by*

UKIP after being filmed in a fly-on-the-wall documentary saying "the only people I do have problems with are negroes".

*

This week's focus groups with undecided voters were held in the Conservative–Labour marginal of Worcester and in Muswell Hill, part of the Hornsey & Wood Green constituency in which Lynne Featherstone finds herself on the Liberal Democrat front line against Labour. She has a fight on her hands, as our polling in the seat has found (and not even the Lib Dems' mysterious private polling claims to contradict) but, on this evidence, if she does lose she should not take it personally.

"I'm on Lynne's mailing list and get her emails," said one participant (everyone called her Lynne – a mark of familiarity generally reserved only for Boris). "She's on the ball and connected to the local area." "I emailed her about a petition," said another. "She replied and explained why we couldn't do the thing we were asking for, and I thought, 'Fair play, I've heard the other side.'" Nearly everyone had received regular letters or literature, and an unusual number had had personal contact during her time as MP: "Lynne has spent time talking to me and came to my door and answered emails." Some had noticed her actions as a minister: "She was in the press for stopping some misogynistic bloke coming to the country because he did a video on how to pick up women. I like that. She's proactive and just does it."

*"The Lib Dems cared about the little people,
the ants on the ground."*

But rather more in sorrow than in anger, most of those who had voted Lib Dem at the last election planned to switch in May. The party had seemed a positive alternative in 2010 ("They cared about the little people, the ants on the ground"), but had disappointed them either by going into coalition in the first place ("I felt duped!") or because they did not seem to have asserted themselves ("I understood why he would join the coalition to try and push through his policies, but he has taken a back seat. I thought he would have more influence over Cameron"; "They used to have gumption but it seems to have dispersed"). The priority for these left-leaning voters, then, was to change the government: "I was upset about the war and other things, so I voted Lib Dem. But now I'm going to be more strategic. I want the Tories out."

> *"I was upset about the war and other things, so I voted Lib Dem. But now I'm going to be more strategic. I want the Tories out."*

Some of those who were unconvinced by Labour were considering the Greens, and the groups had noticed the party's leader "making a shambles" in her LBC radio interview – although, perhaps mercifully, nobody could remember her name ("Bennett, I think. Is it Jane? No, hang on, I'm thinking of *Pride and Prejudice*"). The few who had heard the infamous interview agreed it was excruciating ("It was like a sketch from *The Fast Show*") but for those who had not already dismissed the Green Party, the episode had not dented its appeal: "In some ways it endears me to them a bit more. There is so much pressure and some of them are so slick, and they have their spin doctors. People get flustered, it's human"; "At least it wasn't the usual double-speak. Politicians don't usually answer the question anyway."

*

For our groups, the Straw–Rifkind debacle had joined HSBC and tax avoidance on the list of not particularly staggering stories that were peripheral to the main campaign. Among those who had realised the incident had been a media sting and no money had changed hands (which was by no means everybody: "They've been paid to lobby for the Chinese" was a frequent synopsis), some were surprised that characters of such experience should have fallen for the ruse – which suggested that most of their junior colleagues would have been only too willing to go along with the scheme. Our participants had noticed that the parties had acted quickly to suspend both MPs, but "they had to, to get it off the news".

*

Our groups had also clocked David Cameron's pledge to retain the Winter Fuel Allowance, free bus passes and TV licences for pensioners. As always, for everyone who argued "They've paid their taxes, let them enjoy it," another asked, "If you've got your Jag parked outside, why do you need a Freedom Pass?" The Tories have evidently concluded that the argument is not going to be won on its merits either way and decided to harvest the pensioner votes (which at least everyone could agree was the main reason behind the policy).

> *"The Green leader is called Bennett, I think. Is it Jane?*
> *No, hang on, I'm thinking of* Pride and Prejudice.*"*

Pressed to name one good thing the government had done in the last five years, the groups (after some considerable thought) came up with a longer list than you might have expected. Raising the tax allowance, free school meals, apprenticeships,

Help to Buy, nursery places for two-year-olds, falling unemployment, tackling the deficit, helping the economy out of recession, the welfare cap, low interest rates, cutting Stamp Duty and "managing to hold onto Scotland" all made the list. The "Bedroom Tax" was also put on the good things list as often as it was on the bad things list – which also included cutting the Armed Forces, failing to reduce immigration, "shafting teachers", privatising the Post Office, not dealing properly with the excesses of the financial sector, "blaming people on benefits for the problems of the country" and the amorphous hobgoblin of NHS "privatisation".

The question of what would change under the Labour government that could take over in ten weeks produced even more head scratching. Some more apprenticeships, a Mansion Tax (which one woman, a social worker, said "would give the impression that if you work hard and succeed you will be punished for it"), a higher minimum wage, possibly more house building, and "they might invest more in the NHS to keep it going". Promises that had got through from any party were hard to believe: "I only believe what they say about what they're going to cut." For some, the main thing that would change under Labour would be "the face we see on TV".

*

Partly to counter the idea that nothing would change under a new government, Labour recently produced a short video featuring "101 reasons to vote Labour". The format, with cheery people holding up a succession of placards bearing handwritten Labour pledges, felt "bright, positive, optimistic", as did the musical accompaniment and absence of commentary: "We get enough of politicians talking." But some people – by no means all unsympathetic to Labour – suspected that the "bamboozling" rush of policies projected at a speed too quick to read did not suggest an abundance of good ideas but a dearth: "It's as though they don't want you to read them, just in case."

"101 reasons to vote Labour in 101 seconds"

A Conservative video warned that Miliband posed a threat to the economic recovery

A Conservative video, apparently modelled on a film made for the Australian Liberals, shows a succession of Tory achievements falling and then crashing into the background against a vintage recording of "Wish Me Luck (As You Wave Me Goodbye)". It closes with a picture of the Labour leader and the warning: "Ed Miliband and the economy: Don't risk it." Most people protested about negativity and personalisation and wished the party would say: "This is what we've done, this is what we face, this is our future plan." But one or two of the men admitted they found it "quite powerful. The trouble is, he hasn't got the face."

*

That is all very well, you say, but what if the leaders were holiday destinations? Glad you asked. Mr Cameron, according to our groups, would be "somewhere suave, like Monaco", or, quite possibly, "an offshore island to store your money in". Mr Farage would simply be "Blighty!", probably Margate or Southend because "they adore him down there" or (the view from Muswell Hill) "Benidorm. Somewhere tacky and loud with egg and chips." Mr Clegg would be somewhere "nice and inoffensive", or possibly, since he must feel beleaguered, a distant location like the Caribbean, "where people don't know him so he won't get hassled all the time". Mr Miliband? A place "where the traffic is terrible, because he doesn't have any sense of direction". Alternatively, "the Moon, his own little world", or, more charitably, "somewhere misunderstood – a really nice place but no one goes there".

STEVENAGE AND SOUTHAMPTON
3 & 5 March: 9 weeks to go

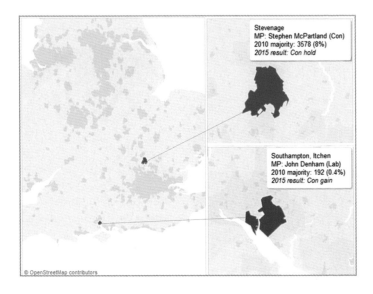

Stevenage
MP: Stephen McPartland (Con)
2010 majority: 3578 (8%)
2015 result: Con hold

Southampton, Itchen
MP: John Denham (Lab)
2010 majority: 192 (0.4%)
2015 result: Con gain

© OpenStreetMap contributors

David Cameron made his "final offer" to the broadcasters, saying he would take part in a single TV debate involving all seven leaders, which must take place before the end of March; this raised the prospect of his being "empty-chaired" in any further debates involving other party leaders in which he refused to take part. The PM also promised to double to 200,000 the number of cut-price new homes in a scheme aimed at first-time buyers aged under forty. Ed Miliband said a Labour government would build 200,000 homes a year by the end of the next parliament. Nigel Farage said he would not make a good Prime Minister and that he does not have a "normal family relationship" because of the pressures of his job.

*

This week's focus groups with undecided voters took place in Stevenage and Southampton, where the election is now firmly on the agenda: "It's even on *Loose Women*. They had that Nigel Farage on today." People in both venues had begun to receive literature, letters, phone calls and visits from canvassers, and most could name their local MP.

Stephen McPartland was well regarded ("He's actually *interested* in Stevenage"), as was John Denham in Southampton, where people praised him for the work he had done locally, but many did not realise he was standing down. Among those who did, a few could name Labour's Rowenna Davis and the Tory Royston Smith. For most participants, though, the decision would rest more on national questions – "the broader spectrum" – than on local issues or candidates.

> *"The election is even on* **Loose** Women. *They had that Nigel Farage on today."*

The groups had noticed the latest frenzy over TV debates, but remained unmoved. In previous rounds, people have said they would watch the debates if they happened, but those most apt to criticise David Cameron for his reluctance to take part were those already least inclined to vote for him. This week, again, we found nothing to suggest Cameron would be seriously damaged if the debates did not go ahead and he was blamed: "He should spend his time running the country rather than standing on stage." Indeed, since the leaders only seem to "act like children" when they get together, the event would probably not be very enlightening anyway.

*

The fact that Labour and the Conservatives had both been "doing housing" had also entered our participants' consciousness, though most were hazy on the details of either party's plan (other than the pledge to build several hundred thousand by some future date) or the difference between the two. However, a few had noted features like the Conservatives' proposed discount scheme for first-time buyers aged under forty, which they welcomed in principle, but even with schemes like this, the idea of themselves or their children owning their own home seemed beyond reach: "People talk about affordable housing but what's affordable about a £250k house when you're on £20k? And how are you going to save a 5 per cent deposit when you're in rented accommodation?"

"Cameron communicates at a number of levels, but with Miliband, it's all up here, talking in theories. You think, 'That's all very well, but it doesn't work like that.'"

Immigration was raised in both venues, most forcefully in Southampton where many regarded it as the most important issue at stake given its effect on local public services ("The population has doubled!"). They also regarded the failure to reduce immigration as the biggest mark against the current government. However, opinion was not all one way. While one taxi driver said his income had been affected by an influx of fifty Romanian competitors, a transport manager said his firm had found it impossible to recruit an HGV driver and had had to look abroad: "Blaming immigration for the problems of the country is not a reasonable thing to do."

Only UKIP were thought to have a clear position on immigration, giving the party an obvious attraction for those who were worried about the subject. Some felt they had bravely raised questions other parties had deliberately ignored: "Two elections ago, there was a consensus not to discuss immigration." But there was concern at the idea of the party's role ever going beyond this: "I like them being in the background and saying it's important to remember these things, but I would be very frightened if they got in or were in control of anything."

For those considering the party, would their decision be affected by the fact they lived in a marginal constituency? "A what, sorry?" Once they realised the result could be very close between Labour and the Conservatives, the Southampton women in particular felt more inclined to revert to their usual party – Labour.

*

However, even those leaning towards Labour were far from sure the party had learned the right lessons from its previous time in government. For some, doubts about Ed Miliband as Prime Minister made the decision a real dilemma. "Cameron communicates at a number of levels, but with Miliband, it's all up here, talking in theories. You think, 'That's all very well, but it doesn't work like that.'" One problem was that "there probably isn't one working-class member of the Labour Party", let alone any of the others. In fact, "none of them has ever done anything proper. They go to university and become career politicians."

Well, then, what jobs would the leaders be best suited to outside politics? Mr Cameron would be a headmaster, or a company director "in charge of things". Mr Farage would almost certainly be a pub landlord, and a good one at that, or would run his own small but successful business. The groups struggled to place Mr Clegg in the outside world: probably something administrative or perhaps a supermarket store manager. Mr Miliband's ideal job – and this from people who did not know of his previous career – was to be a university professor. Make of that what you will.

NORTHAMPTON AND CARDIFF
10 & 12 March: 8 weeks to go

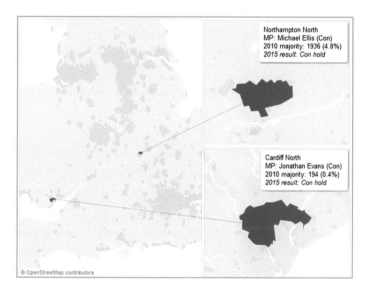

Northampton North
MP: Michael Ellis (Con)
2010 majority: 1936 (4.8%)
2015 result: Con hold

Cardiff North
MP: Jonathan Evans (Con)
2010 majority: 194 (0.4%)
2015 result: Con hold

© OpenStreetMap contributors

Labour claimed that the Tories were planning "extreme and risky" public spending cuts of £70 billion, which would leave Britain with "the smallest army since Cromwell". The Conservatives launched a poster featuring a diminutive Ed Miliband in the pocket of Alex Salmond's jacket. David Cameron said a Conservative government would open 500 new free schools by 2020. A poll found majorities thinking Cameron was cowardly for his reluctance to take part in TV debates, and that they should go ahead even if he declined to take part.

*

This week's focus groups with undecided voters took place in Northampton and Cardiff. Campaigning is evidently well under way in both locations, with most participants having received direct mail and leaflets, or spotted items on Facebook, increasingly used as a campaigning tool and source of news. The Cardiff groups reported that Conservative candidate Craig Williams has alighted on a novel way of getting people to read his letters, apparently addressing them as "Dear Lovely Resident". It made them smile, which is a good start.

"Cameron has got more arrogant as time has gone on, and the debates are proof."

As far as our groups were concerned, the most prominent election news story was still "this incessant thing about debates". The most politically engaged participants were not surprisingly the most put out at the prospect of being denied the spectacle, and those who already took a dim view of David Cameron saw his position as part of a pattern of behaviour: "He has got more arrogant as time has gone on, and the debates are proof."

But from others there were signs that the mood was moving from indifference to annoyance that more important issues were not being discussed: "It's just hyped up by the media. What about the rest of the country and what's happening?" People also felt they were unlikely to learn much if debates went ahead, particularly if all seven leaders took part: "It would be an act, like Prime Minister's Questions, a shouting contest. They never answer the question, just tell you what you want to hear, then let you down anyway."

*

Labour's claims that a new Conservative government would make £70 billion of cuts, resulting in "catastrophic" reductions in services and the smallest army since Cromwell, had registered with some participants. Even those who had had enough of austerity thought this sounded a bit on the hyperbolic side, and made Labour's charge less believable rather than more devastating: "I can't believe they would seriously compromise the safety of the country. I can't believe they would be stupid enough."

In Cardiff, discussion of austerity led to the question of the NHS in Wales, which most agreed was in trouble. Though they realised responsibility for health was devolved, few thought the Labour-run Welsh government was mainly to blame, since decisions about funding must surely be made in London: "Who has the final say? It's the money, isn't it?"

*

Vote Conservative ✗

The Tories' claim that the SNP would influence Miliband as PM featured heavily in the campaign

Some in the groups had seen the Conservative poster featuring a tiny Ed Miliband tucked into Alex Salmond's jacket pocket.

It raised a chuckle and a few agreed that it would be a terrible thing for the SNP to be calling the shots at Westminster ("There would be another farcical independence vote. You've made your decision, get on with it"). But most were unmoved by the argument – after all, what were they supposed to do about it? If they wanted Labour in government, they would vote Labour, and if they didn't, they wouldn't – they could not affect the shape of any coalition once their ballots were cast: "It's going to be messy whatever happens."

> *"Cameron hasn't knackered things up any further than they already were, so credit for that."*

For some in our groups, the Conservatives were beyond consideration ("I've had four years of pay cuts and I'm losing benefits"); these people were in two minds between Labour and UKIP. Those still weighing the Tories up tended to think Cameron was the most convincing leader ("He hasn't knackered things up any further than they already were, so credit for that") but wanted to know what they would do on immigration, the NHS, and ensuring corporations paid their fair share in tax. They were depressed by the prospect of perpetual austerity ("What sort of state is the country in if we can't afford lollipop ladies?") and wanted a reason to believe that if the economy was recovering, things would be better for them, not just other people: "The cinemas are packed and people are out and about, but for the people I speak to, life is getting harder. Shopping has gone through the roof … We need to see the reward in things like pay."

Some were also doubtful about the idea of re-electing the Conservatives to "finish the job": "How can you finish the job of running the country? Are they suddenly going to say, 'There, we've finished,' and disappear down the pub?"

"What sort of state is the country in if we can't even afford lollipop ladies?"

On the whole, people were glad to have UKIP around to stir things up. But some were worried about a "racist undertone" and wanted reassuring that "the atrocious things some of their people come out with" did not give a true picture of the party. Interestingly, a number of participants said their school-age children had been horrified to hear they were even considering UKIP: "My eleven-year-old son said, 'You can't vote that, that's racist'"; "My boy is mixed race. He just looked at me in astonishment." There was also the familiar concern that "we need to look at the whole manifesto, but that's the problem with UKIP, they haven't got one".

Even so, Nigel Farage had more admirers than detractors. Though a few thought he was "along for the ride, to make a name for himself", more thought he was the most honest politician of the time: "He even said he would never be PM because he would be rubbish at it. That was fantastic." Others were in two minds: "He's either an evil genius or a fairly normal bloke."

"How can you finish the job of running the country?
Are they suddenly going to say, 'There, we've finished,'
and disappear down the pub?"

None of our participants was seriously considering the Liberal Democrats, even in Northampton where the party had come a very close third in 2010. "They're not in the running. I voted for them last time because I thought they were like Labour used to be – a social moral conscience with a bit of common sense. But now ... they've lost their purpose."

*

Labour seemed to lack a clear purpose and a credible plan, as well as a persuasive campaign ("Margaret Thatcher wouldn't have been dicking around with a pink bus," as a young primary-school teacher and self-professed feminist put it). "They're so staid. They need revamping."

"Margaret Thatcher wouldn't have been dicking around with a pink bus."

A few praised Ed Miliband for being "for the people" and against privatisation, or even thought he had, in recent months, become "stronger and more believable; more determined". But for others who wanted to vote Labour, he made it more difficult for them to do so: "He's not a complete block but it's not helping things"; "He doesn't inspire confidence. In fact, it frightens me, the idea of him being in charge." Some also disliked what they saw as his political instincts: "He wants to appeal to the lowest common denominator. If someone gets something because they work hard, he wants to take it off them and give it to someone else."

"If someone gets something because they work hard, Miliband wants to take it off them and give it to someone else."

Still, in terms of background and personal experience, people thought there was little to choose between the three established party leaders: "They're all Oxford types anyway." For them, this divide between the millionaire insider and the ordinary voter was more significant than any political distinction between the three. And this was before news had emerged that the Milibands possessed a greater than average number of kitchens.

"Farage is either an evil genius or a fairly normal bloke."

Despite this, if each of the leaders found themselves with the unexpected luxury of a free Friday night, they would not necessarily all spend it in the same way, according to our groups. Mr Farage would inevitably go to the pub, possibly after a spot of fishing, or, for the cynics, "to a French restaurant with his German wife to complain about immigration". Mr Clegg, a likeable "family man", would take his wife and children ten-pin bowling, or stay in with them to watch *Bake Off*. Mr Miliband, if he did not have a "posh dinner party" planned, would be playing with the train set some suspect he has in his loft, or spend the time "reading the opinion polls for something to grab onto" (though the disparagers didn't have much conviction here: of course he would make the most of extra time with his family). Mr Cameron, meanwhile, would "get a helicopter to Cornwall" with Sam and the kids, where he would take the country air to help him focus on the job. Should the family be away, however, he would go "to his club" to engage in "mildly inappropriate banter with Conservative MPs and eight bottles of Cabernet Sauvignon".

LEAMINGTON AND DEWSBURY
17 & 19 March: 7 weeks to go

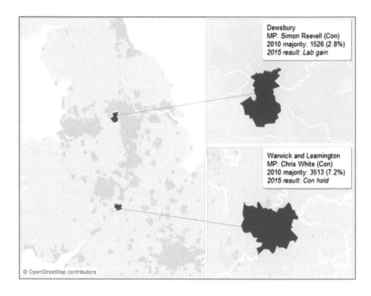

Dewsbury
MP: Simon Reevell (Con)
2010 majority: 1526 (2.8%)
2015 result: Lab gain

Warwick and Leamington
MP: Chris White (Con)
2010 majority: 3513 (7.2%)
2015 result: Con hold

© OpenStreetMap contributors

George Osborne delivered the final Budget of the coalition govern-
ment, including an increase in the tax-free personal allowance to
£11,000 by 2017, a new Help to Buy ISA to help first-time home-
buyers save for a deposit, cancellation of the fuel duty increase that
had been planned for September, a reduction in beer duty and
measures to allow pensioners to sell their annuity for a cash lump
sum. Labour unveiled their five election pledges: "A strong economic
foundation, higher living standards for working families, an NHS
with time to care, controls on immigration, a country where the
next generation can do better than the last." Negotiations over
the format of leaders' TV debates continued between the parties and

the broadcasters. Ed Miliband ruled out forming a coalition with the SNP. He was photographed for a newspaper interview in what turned out to be the smaller of the two kitchens in his London house.

*

In this week's focus groups, news of the decision at hand had filtered through to most of our undecided voters, if not all ("When *is* the next general election?" asked one fellow conversationally, as though discussing leap years or the Olympic Games). One sternly reminded the group about the importance of turning out on the day: "If you're registered and you don't vote, your vote goes to the party in power." Puzzled looks all round. "Is that not right? I've been told that for years." Oddly enough, this is not the first time we have heard this said in our research. Where do these ideas come from?

*

On Tuesday evening in Leamington, none of our participants had realised that the following day was Budget day. Some lamented that the event had lost its old magic: "Years ago you would sit around the telly and watch it. Then you used to drive to the petrol station and fill your tank before the tax went up." Nobody expected anything concrete that would affect them, except perhaps the usual niggling tax hike on life's small pleasures ("I work hard for my cigarettes!").

But on the Thursday in Dewsbury, it was clear that some of the announcements had got through to our swing voters, at least temporarily. Several said there had been more positive things in the Budget than they had expected. People spontaneously mentioned the higher income tax threshold, the petrol duty freeze, the penny off beer, the minimum wage rise and – especially – the new savings scheme for first-time buyers. A number of people had noted the details of the Help to Buy ISA, which is unusual for a policy announcement of any kind, and planned to take advantage of it.

Even so, there was scepticism on some fronts: the planned increase in the tax threshold for 2017 "leaves plenty of time for them to change their minds", and for some, the concern was "more what they didn't talk about. He didn't mention the NHS at all." Several were also doubtful about the Chancellor's sunny picture of the economy, and particularly the number of zero-hour contracts hidden in the job creation figures: "Unemployment is down drastically, but is it meaningful employment?"

> *"I don't think I'm going to vote. And to think what the suffragettes went through."*

The groups were shown Labour's five headline election pledges ("A strong economic foundation, higher living standards for working families, an NHS with the time to care, controls on immigration, a country where the next generation can do better than the last"). They were presented unlabelled, so to speak, alongside the six Conservative themes launched in January ("Dealing with the economic deficit, creating jobs, lowering taxes, improving education, tackling housing shortages, helping the retired"). As often as not, people associated the pledge or theme with the wrong party: *"A strong economic foundation. That's Tory. I can just see David Cameron mouthing those words."* The apparent interchangeability of the parties' priorities led to confusion bordering on despair among some participants ("I don't think I'm going to vote. And to think what the suffragettes went through"). However, a few thought they detected a pattern: "That's Labour isn't it [it was], because it looks like they're spending a lot of money".

The details of Labour's pledges – including twenty-five hours' free childcare, 20,000 more nurses, 8,000 more GPs and a cut in tuition fees – sounded appealing to many in the groups but provoked the familiar suspicions. In particular, they doubted the statement in the first pledge that none of Labour's manifesto commitments require additional borrowing. "It's what everyone wants but I really don't know how we can afford to do it"; "Just recently they were reporting that there are not enough GPs. How can we suddenly have them? It takes years to train a GP"; "I see hidden taxes and debt going back up. How much interest are we paying already?"

*

News of a politician having two kitchens had reached the groups, albeit through what appeared in some cases to be a series of Chinese whispers. "David Cameron did that photo in his huge kitchen for his Christmas cards that he sent to his friends, and then he did that election photo in the tiny kitchen where the servants make tea." That was Ed Miliband, someone pointed out. "Well, there you are. That's why I'm voting UKIP."

This echoed the more serious point that "MPs complain that they struggle to get by on seventy grand a year. They don't seem to realise people are struggling to get by on £7 an hour."

> *"At least the Tories say they're going to screw you*
> *and then they screw you."*

Reservations about each of the parties are now well embedded and look unlikely to change in the next six weeks. Doubts about Labour were evident from the discussion about their pledges, and the trouble with Ed Miliband is that "he doesn't make you think anything after you've watched him".

The Lib Dems' party-political broadcast had been "laughable – Clegg was making all these promises and I thought, 'Well, you didn't do naff all last time.'"

Some thought David Cameron was "a bit Jeremy Clarkson" (in a bad way, apparently), although "I believe him more than I believe any of the others". Some were wary of the Conservatives for deep-rooted historical reasons ("The miners and s***. That was pretty hard core"), though, on the upside, with their austerity plans you knew what you were going to get: "At least the Tories say they are going to screw you and then they screw you."

For all UKIP's virtues, "they want to close the border, but I'd like to be able to work abroad", and again some worried that "they're like a sly version of the BNP", and that, while "Farage has the image of the beer-swilling man of the people, there are plenty of issues in the background that they don't talk about that would come through if they ever got close to power".

As for the Greens ("bless them"): "Where have they been for the last five years? Are they a competitor?"

*

One aspect of the contest that some feel has received too little attention is this: if each of the leaders were a band or singer, which band or singer would they be? Mr Miliband would be something inoffensive but perhaps not entirely current – Wham, say, or Daniel O'Donnell. Mr Clegg? Something middle-of-the-road – the Lighthouse Family or Simply Red, or Cliff Richard, who "pops up at Christmas then goes back down again" , or "someone's sidekick, like Sonny in Sonny and Cher". Mr Cameron was harder to place: Take That ("He'd be Gary Barlow"), Coldplay, Justin Bieber or Keith Urban – though some saw him as Simon Cowell, the impresario rather than the performer. No such ambiguity with Mr Farage, though: three of our four groups spontaneously said he would be Johnny Rotten or the Sex Pistols ("He just wants to swear and drink beer and wee all over people"). That or The Wurzels.

WOLVERHAMPTON AND CHEADLE
24 & 26 March: 6 weeks to go

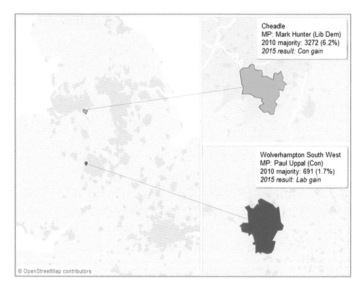

Cheadle
MP: Mark Hunter (Lib Dem)
2010 majority: 3272 (6.2%)
2015 result: Con gain

Wolverhampton South West
MP: Paul Uppal (Con)
2010 majority: 691 (1.7%)
2015 result: Lab gain

© OpenStreetMap contributors

David Cameron ruled out serving as PM *for a third parliament, observing in a* TV *interview that "terms are like Shredded Wheat – two are wonderful but three might just be too many". Labour launched a poster to highlight their claims on Tory spending plans with the headline: "Next time, they'll cut to the bone." In the last session of Prime Minister's Questions before the election, Ed Miliband asked Cameron if he would rule out an increase in* VAT; *the* PM *surprised him by answering "Yes."*

*

This week's focus groups with undecided voters took place in Wolverhampton and Cheadle. Participants said they were receiving a steady supply of campaign literature, not that they seemed very impressed. "I filled in a Labour questionnaire about my three main issues and now all I get is emails and phone calls asking if I'll deliver leaflets"; "I had one saying our MP had done this, this and this – which did I think was best?" There was also a reminder of the old campaigning truth that you can't fatten the pig on market day: "Why do they only pop up six weeks before the election? When they send a community newsletter that's quite interesting, where they say what they're doing and there are pictures and things you can relate to."

This is part of the local strategy upon which the Liberal Democrats have long relied, with great success. However, their greater national role has complicated the relationship with local voters: while some give them credit for having "tempered the right-wing nut side of the Conservative Party", others said they would now think more widely: "The Lib Dems were always known to have done a good job in the area. It's when they go into national things that they're not so good. I'm happy with Mark Hunter [the current Lib Dem MP] but now I'm thinking I've got to look at the national picture too, the bigger picture."

> *"There must be a hidden agenda somewhere.*
> *Is the idea that Boris is going to come in?"*

Most people had noticed that David Cameron had ruled out a third term as Prime Minister. Only those already the least favourable to him saw this as arrogant ("He's already thinking, 'I've got this one, I'm thinking about the next one'"). Others were puzzled by it. The statement was probably calculated

("He's got to have known they were going to make a fuss about it") but to what end they were not sure, since they did not think it put him in a very good light: "He has got a responsibility to all of us and if he's already thinking about leaving, why should we think he's committed to looking after us all? It looks as though he's thinking to the next stage ahead once he's gone."

It also opened the troubling question of the succession: "He is planting that seed that he is leaving so you're asking who will be next"; "There must be a hidden agenda somewhere. Is the idea that Boris is going to come in?" None of those who were seriously considering voting Conservative said Cameron's statement would be enough in itself to put them off, but many were unsettled and above all surprised by it: "I would have thought he'd keep his mouth shut."

*

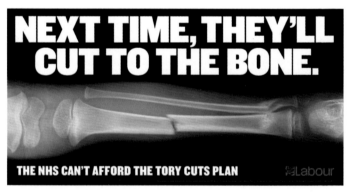

Labour claimed the Conservatives would implement devastating public spending cuts

Labour's poster warning of future Conservative austerity, which declares "Next time they'll cut to the bone – the NHS can't afford the Tory cuts plan", was best received by those already leaning towards Labour, or at least away from the Conservatives. For these people, the message resonated with what they already thought.

However, it could only work for those inclined to believe that the Tories would cut more than they had to, not just because circumstances forced them to balance the books. There were some takers for this view: "It's ideological. Peeling back the state, the 'I'm alright, stuff you' attitude."

For most others: "There's no substance, it's just a statement. There's no evidence. I'm sure the Conservatives have said they're not going to touch the NHS, unless I've heard wrong. Labour are just hoping people will take [the poster] at face value." (Even so, said one Tory sympathiser of the austerity programme, "The Conservatives could market it better and not look so proud about it. 'Another £30 billion! This is great fun!'") The poster seems designed to galvanise existing Labour support, in which case it is doing its job.

"The Conservatives could market austerity better and not look so proud about it. 'Another £30 billion! This is great fun!'"

But discussion about the prospect of future cuts revealed some confusion about the need for austerity, and particularly the difference between the debt and the deficit: "They have said we need to cut deeper, but the national debt has gone up, apparently. So why have there been cuts? I don't mind cuts if the debt's not going up, but…" And if things are so good, why are they so bad? "We're supposed to be out of recession. I don't understand why we've got so much debt. They don't explain it properly. With the taxes we pay, you think, how much do they want to drain us?"

*

The groups had registered the parties' skirmish over VAT and some had even clocked the PMQs exchange in which Cameron seemed to flummox Ed Miliband by ruling out a rise. A few thought Labour deserved credit for extracting the pledge from the PM: "Miliband almost forced him to say it. Did he just say it to shut them up?" Others were amused by the spectacle – "Ed was done up like a kipper, and then he couldn't answer on National Insurance" – but nobody found the episode very enlightening. They felt none the wiser about the parties' plans or how they would be paid for: "Tell us what you are going to do!" Not for the first time, the absence of any substantial ideas – at least that they had noticed – was what most characterised the groups' view of the campaign.

*

That being the case, people had to fall back on their view of what the parties were really like. One question – if each party were a house, what kind of house would it be? – gave some interesting pointers. In fact, the groups offered some remarkably specific answers. The Labour house is in a terrace, with the front door leading straight onto the pavement. Hi-vis jackets hang in the hallway, and people in the living room are watching their 50-inch plasma TV and eating cottage pie with chips and beer. "The furniture is nice, but it's all on HP."

The Conservative house has nice thick carpets and "one of those kitchen islands". There are Hunter wellies in the hall and a "posh dog", probably a chocolate Labrador. But "you can't get to the door because there is an intercom at the gates", and once inside "you have to wipe your feet".

The Lib Dem house is in a cul-de-sac. There are sandals by the door and solar panels on the roof. This house is also home to a dog ("a mongrel from the rescue centre") that would be allowed to jump on the sofa. The décor is either plain and beige or "quite odd", having been chosen by "trendy intellectuals".

The UKIP house is "a bit Hyacinth Bucket" and has "a wrought-iron fence all round it to keep everyone out". There is a flagpole in the garden and the local hunt is gathering outside. The ageing residents (who "don't get on with their neighbours because they are a different colour") are smoking heavily and "talking about how it was in their day". The timer on the stereo is set to play the national anthem every day at noon.

THURROCK AND BRENTFORD
31 March & 1 April: 5 weeks to go

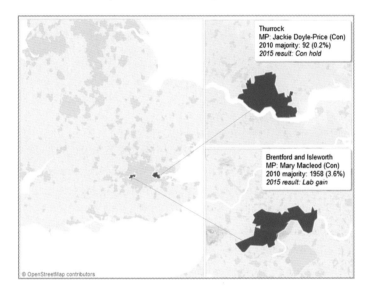

Thurrock
MP: Jackie Doyle-Price (Con)
2010 majority: 92 (0.2%)
2015 result: Con hold

Brentford and Isleworth
MP: Mary Macleod (Con)
2010 majority: 1958 (3.6%)
2015 result: Lab gain

© OpenStreetMap contributors

Agreement was reached on the leaders' TV debates; the first programme was broadcast, in which David Cameron and Ed Miliband were separately interviewed by Jeremy Paxman and questioned by a studio audience. Asked if he was tough enough to be Prime Minister, Miliband replied "Hell yes I'm tough enough." Parliament was dissolved. Cameron warned of the "stark choice" voters faced between himself and Miliband as PM. A letter to the Daily Telegraph *from senior executives of more than a hundred large companies expressed support for Conservative economic policies and warned that a Labour government would "threaten jobs and deter investment". A Labour advertisement in the* Financial

Times *quoted business leaders warning of the consequences of Britain leaving the European Union. The actor Martin Freeman presented a Labour election broadcast in which he said he would vote for the party because of its values of "community, compassion, decency". New data showed higher* GDP, *rising consumer confidence and improved living standards, prompting George Osborne to hail a "hat-trick" of good economic news.* UKIP *launched their pledge card: "Say no to the* EU; *Control our borders; Extra £3 billion for the* NHS; *Cut foreign aid spending; No tax on the minimum wage."*

*

Despite the parties' frenetic activity since the start of the year, for some of our participants in Thurrock and Brentford the real action seemed hardly to have started: "It feels like the start of a boxing match where they strut round the ring bigging themselves up." Local street campaigners are out in force, however. While some in the groups confessed to peeking from upstairs curtains to avoid opening the door to a canvasser, there was still an appetite for the traditional doorstep conversation: "You can send me bits of paper all you like, but I've got questions. You can't ask a piece of paper questions. Knock on my door!"

*

There were complaints, as ever, that coverage of the campaign was still dominated by process stories rather than anything they felt could help them towards a decision: "The thing I find frustrating is that all the talk is about whether he's going to do a third term and who is going to turn up to the debates. I don't care about all that, I want to know who I'm voting for."

"Labour want to put more money into everything. But if they're asked how they're going to do it they just say 'Tory cuts!'"

Even so, some issues had begun to get through. The Conservatives had been heard on the economy, help for first-time buyers and the deficit (although "they never tell you how well we're doing. Every now and then you get a statement from the bank manager saying, 'You've paid this much off, well done,' but with the deficit they bamboozle you and don't say it in plain English"); Labour on zero-hour contracts, raising the minimum wage, the NHS and wanting "to put more money into everything. But if they're asked how they're going to do it they just say 'Tory cuts!' I don't know how they are going to put more into public services *and* cut the deficit."

*

Labour launched their short campaign by warning of the dangers of leaving the EU

Some had noticed the letter from 100 business leaders supporting Conservative economic policies, and rather fewer had heard about Labour's FT ad quoting business support for staying in the EU (which most seemed to think an odd priority for the party to have launched its campaign with).

A few thought business endorsements lent extra credibility to the government, but more often the discussion led back to the question of who was benefiting from the economic recovery and the policies that gave rise to it (if any: several felt that since the country had been emerging from financial crisis and recession, it would have been going some to make things any worse). People were still finding things hard – "Utility bills are horrendous. If they've gone down I haven't noticed" – and if anyone was better off it was probably people at the top end, such as those who might sign business leaders' letters to the *Telegraph*.

The "hat-trick of good news" on GDP, disposable income and consumer confidence received the same downbeat reception from most: "I just feel nothing has changed for years."

*

David Cameron's video setting out the choice to be made at the election – a condensed version of his statement in Downing Street on the dissolution of parliament – was given much the same reaction, especially on the claim that the country was growing strongly and creating jobs ("A lot of them are zero hours, or part time, or minimum wage, not careers").

The attempt to frame the choice as being between himself and Miliband also underlined how sensitive people are to anything that sounds remotely like an attack and how quickly it can obscure more positive parts of the message ("They always degrade other parties rather than talk about what they're going to do"). There was also resistance to the idea of a straightforward choice: "He says it's between the two parties, but it's not actually. Like it or not, UKIP and the SNP are there and they might have an impact on the outcome."

*

In a Labour broadcast, Martin Freeman talked about "community, compassion, decency"

The Labour broadcast starring Martin Freeman brought a starkly different response in our two locations. To the Brentford group the message sounded "warm", "genuine", "heartfelt" ("apart from when he was talking about what the Conservatives would do; that felt a bit speculative"), and those already more sympathetic to Labour responded to what they heard as the appeal to social conscience.

But the theme of contrasting values cut less ice in Thurrock: "It's all well and good to say, 'We're nice people and we care about you more,' but I want someone who can sort out the country." It failed to answer the doubts people had about Labour: "He doesn't tell you where they're going to make cuts.

If they're going to do the things he said, where's the money coming from?" "I just think about last time they were in and made a mess of it." For some, the fact that Freeman was fronting the film told its own story: "Ed Miliband wouldn't do it because he couldn't carry it off, because he's not believable." Some also had trouble suspending their disbelief: "He's a very, very good actor. It's just another role to him."

"It's all well and good to say, 'We're nice people and we care about you more,' but I want someone who can sort out the country."

People in both venues debated the Miliband factor. Most agreed that he would line up less well against Obama, Merkel and Putin than Cameron does. How important is it to have someone who can hold their own on the international stage? Less so, perhaps not surprisingly, to those already leaning most towards Labour (as one put it, "It would be nice, but it's not a deal-breaker").

Some also thought Miliband was starting to make a better impression in his media appearances, and had done well in the non-debate, even though the interview had unfairly "spent five minutes talking about his brother" (a perfect piece of voter contrariness, incidentally: ask people what they think of Ed and as often as not someone will still say, "They chose the wrong Miliband").

"The SNP wanted independence, and now they want to say what goes on."

Several people in both constituencies spontaneously said they were worried about "a Labour administration under the fist of the Scottish MPs". They were annoyed that the SNP should be in a position to determine the shape of the government ("They didn't want anything to do with it, they wanted independence, and now they want to say what goes on") and troubled by the potential consequences: "They don't like us. How much more money are we going to have to push up north? They're not for our interests."

*

UKIP's pledge card

The UKIP campaign was clearly making itself felt in Thurrock, more so than the other parties': "Tim Aker is all about local issues. I must get something from them three or four times a week." One also reported that the party's message was an inversion of the usual Tory appeal: "The UKIP leaflets say a vote for the Conservatives in Thurrock would let Labour in." Though many of our participants were seriously considering voting UKIP, their concerns echoed those heard elsewhere: "All

I can tell you is that they want the immigrants out. What's their policy on the NHS?"

At first glance, the UKIP pledge card was appealing ("Say no to the EU; Control our borders; Extra £3 billion for the NHS; Cut foreign aid spending; No tax on minimum wage"), and seemed a refreshing contrast with what they were hearing from elsewhere: "If they stick to it that's exactly what we want to hear. We're not going to hear that from Labour." Yet for all the dislike of politicians' caveats and evasions, some found this a bit too simplistic to be credible: "It sounds great but it's like when you read an ad and look for the small print. There is no small print, that's the worry."

> *"All I can tell you about UKIP is that they want the immigrants out. What's their policy on the NHS?"*

But those who would end up voting for UKIP would not be looking for a full programme for government but a way of making themselves heard. Often these individuals were wrestling with a dilemma that they did not expect to solve before 7 May: "A vote for UKIP would be a drop in a very big ocean, but I want to give a kick up the backside to the main parties. The Conservatives are better at housekeeping, but I don't feel I'm going to get listened to. I don't think I will decide until the day, and I think a lot of people think like that."

> *"The Conservatives are better at housekeeping, but I don't feel I'm going to get listened to. I don't think I will decide until the day."*

Part of the problem for them was that, as we have heard elsewhere, many think the parties and leaders seem to have more in common with each other than any of them do with people like themselves. Asked where they thought David Cameron would go on an evening out, the answers were predictable enough: somewhere "flash but discreet" for foie gras and chateaubriand with expensive wine poured from a decanter.

So what about Ed Miliband? "Exactly the same. They haven't grafted. They've been lucky, privileged. They're all public schoolboys." Miliband went to a comprehensive, as it happens. "Did he really? Well, he's a millionaire. I imagine his family has got money." Others struggled with the idea of Miliband going out to enjoy himself: "I can't imagine him in a pub. He doesn't strike me as someone who ever goes out or has the slightest bit of fun, ever."

How about Nick Clegg? "He has to stay at home. His wife won't let him out because he has to do the dishes. She's super fierce." Nevertheless, he was "the most normal, as much as they can be", and the one of the four that people would most like to spend the evening with.

Nigel Farage, if not in his usual pub, would go "to Brick Lane for a curry. But he won't tell anyone."

HOYLAKE
9 April: 4 weeks to go

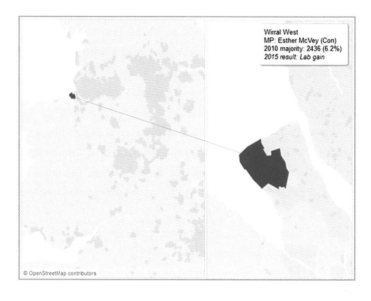

Wirral West
MP: Esther McVey (Con)
2010 majority: 2436 (6.2%)
2015 result: Lab gain

© OpenStreetMap contributors

David Cameron, Ed Miliband, Nick Clegg, Nigel Farage, Natalie Bennett, Nicola Sturgeon and Leanne Wood took part in the first leaders' TV debate. Miliband announced that a Labour government would abolish "non-dom" tax status. Defence Secretary Michael Fallon wrote in The Times *that Labour would be prepared to negotiate away Britain's nuclear deterrent in return for SNP support: "Ed Miliband stabbed his brother in the back to become Labour leader. Now he is willing to stab the United Kingdom in the back to become Prime Minister." Miliband said Fallon was "a decent person" who had "demeaned himself and demeaned his office". The Green Party launched a campaign video depicting the*

Tory, Labour, Lib Dem and UKIP *leaders as members of a boy band in "party political harmony" with indistinguishable policies, and invited viewers to "change the tune".*

*

This week's focus groups with undecided voters took place in the constituency of Wirral West, where Esther McVey is facing a tough campaign to hold her seat. She is battling valiantly, according to our participants, and has made her presence felt consistently, not just at election times: "She seems to knock on my door practically every week." Indeed, all parties seem to have been active: "We often get those *Focus* leaflets from the Lib Dems. You know the sort of thing, a picture of a local councillor standing next to some dog poo." But for all Esther's virtues as a local MP, most said national issues would dominate their decision.

> *"We often get those* **Focus** *leaflets from the Lib Dems. You know the sort of thing, a picture of a local councillor standing next to some dog poo."*

Most people had not seen the seven-way leaders' debates, and the format ("a bit too chaotic") meant most of those who had did not feel they had learned much, other than that Nicola Sturgeon was "one to watch". This was said with a mixture of admiration and suspicion. The SNP leader was generally seen as the most impressive performer, particularly by the women: "She took the lead." But the prospect of her party taking a leading role in Westminster after the election was troubling for some, and the debate over Trident brought this into focus.

The issue had not been much on the minds of any of our participants, but nearly all found the prospect of weakening

Britain's nuclear defence disturbing: "It feels scary that we've got them but possibly even more scary if we don't have them and other counties do"; "They're expensive but we've got Russians coming into our air space and flying in our face ... I wouldn't trust Putin, would you?"

*

Nobody spontaneously mentioned non-doms, though the subject had dominated the news the previous day ("Was it in the *Mail*?"). Labour's approach sounded right to the groups in principle, and nobody was shocked that Labour had proposed the policy or that the Tories had criticised it. When was the last time anyone could remember a politician saying or doing anything that surprised them? "When Margaret Thatcher burst into tears in the car when she was ousted."

*

The Greens' film claimed the Tories, Labour, the Lib Dems and UKIP *were "the one true coalition"*

The Greens Party's boy-band broadcast, which some had seen ("Don't make me watch it again!") provoked everything from broad smiles to frowns of bemusement, though many recognised the central argument that the main parties seemed depressingly similar. Still, this did not seem such a bad thing when they heard the list of what they regarded as wildly expensive and unrealistic Green proposals at the end, including nationalising the railways and scrapping tuition fees. "It gets your attention because it's daft. But at the end when she says what they're going to do, you know the only way to do it is to tax us to death … It's all got to come from somewhere and it comes from us." The threat was not unduly worrying, however: "They can say it because they haven't got a cat in hell's chance."

*

If the Greens (and UKIP) want the election to be about the same old parties versus outsiders who speak for the people, and the Conservatives want it to be about Cameron versus Miliband and competence versus chaos, and Labour want it to be about values, how did the groups themselves characterise the choice at hand?

Often it was about direction, or security versus risk. In general, this view of things favoured the Tories: "It's about keeping us steady and not falling behind"; "They haven't done everything right but they're moving in the right direction." But several who took this view were nonetheless uneasy about it, either because of particular policies they disliked or because they were just not comfortable with the idea of voting Conservative: "The Tories would probably keep the economy steadier but when it boils down to the individual bits and bobs, like tuition fees, you don't like it"; "I did one of those anonymous survey things about which policies you prefer and surprisingly it said I should vote Tory. But I don't know if I could."

"I did one of those anonymous survey things about which policies you prefer and surprisingly it said I should vote Tory. But I don't know if I could."

Most of these people would happily vote Labour were it not for the risk they thought was attached: "Values are nice but it can all go horribly wrong, can't it?" Usually the risk was seen in economic terms: "In 2008, I was made redundant; in 2010, I became self-employed and things are going OK. I don't want to go backwards"; "There is a lot flying around about wage rises, which we couldn't afford. We've got two shops and lots of staff, and we've got to keep the business going." And, as one man put it, a previously Labour-voting retired panel beater, "The risk is Labour starting again as a sort of apprenticeship scheme. Cameron looks like he knows where he's going." But the economy was not the only risk with Labour: "There's the Scottish problem. And … him." What is the problem with "him"? "He just doesn't look like a leader." What does he look like, then? "Parker. The driver from *Thunderbirds*."

The risks were not all in one direction, however, particularly if there was a chance the Tories could be governing on their own: "You've got to remember we've had a Conservative–Lib Dem coalition. If we just had the Conservatives, they might be a bit more extreme." One specific risk was the prospect of an EU referendum and its potential consequences: "The referendum worries me. It just creates a load of ill feeling and tension with Europe. It's a gamble because the Conservatives are committed to that. It could end up like Scotland where everyone is blasé and then suddenly it's 'Blimey, we might lose.'"

"Cameron is not a textbook Tory, not a pompous git."

What if the leaders were to come over for dinner? An evening with Mr Farage would be amusing, and his conversation perhaps "a bit close to the bone". They would cook him roast beef and Yorkshire pudding, or bangers and mash. Would he bring a gift? "A big pack of ciggies."

Mr Clegg would bring a bottle of Chablis (spontaneous unanimity across both groups on this point) and flowers. The groups would give him salmon ("pink and flaky") or "a family barbecue to cheer him up". Of the four, "he would be the most interested in your family, and would ask lots of questions".

Who would Mr Miliband bring with him? "Two advisers." Would he bring a gift? "One of his advisers would have sorted something out." His conversation would either be "very intense", or "he would tell knock-knock jokes".

Mr Cameron would arrive "holding hands tightly" with Sam. Like his deputy, he would enjoy a barbecue (though with steak, rather than the usual burgers and sausages), or something Italian, and would bring good red wine. The conversation? "You wouldn't get an answer on anything serious but you could talk to him. He's not a textbook Tory, not a pompous git.'

ST AUSTELL AND PLYMOUTH
14 & 15 April: 3 weeks to go

Plymouth, Moor View
MP: Alison Seabeck (Lab)
2010 majority: 1588 (3.8%)
2015 result: Con gain

St Austell and Newquay
MP: Stephen Gilbert (Lib Dem)
2010 majority: 1312 (2.8%)
2015 result: Con gain

© OpenStreetMap contributors

The parties launched their election manifestos. The Conservatives promised "strong leadership; a clear economic plan; a brighter, more secure future", and David Cameron described the Tories as "the party of working people". Labour declared that "Britain only succeeds when working people succeed", and Ed Miliband said every policy in his manifesto was funded and would be paid for without additional borrowing. Nick Clegg said the Lib Dems would stop a future administration cutting too much or borrowing too much; his party would "add a heart to a Conservative government and a brain to a Labour one". The UKIP manifesto was titled "Believe in Britain"; Nigel Farage highlighted plans for an Australian-style

points system and proposals to ban foreign criminals from entering
or remaining in the UK.

*

This week's focus groups with undecided voters took place in St Austell, where the incumbent Liberal Democrats face a strong challenge from the Conservatives, and Plymouth, with participants from the Moor View constituency where our polling has found UKIP as the main opponents for Labour *[though in the event the Conservatives gained the seat at the 2015 election]*. Plymouth was also the only venue so far in which we have come across a 'Vote Communist' billboard.

The St Austell participants recognised the constituency as having been a yellow stronghold ("The Lib Dems are *all over* the place") and many had previously voted Lib Dem because of good local MPs. Stephen Gilbert? "David Penhaligon." Most thought Mr Gilbert had stepped into the tradition of standing up for the area: "The pasty tax, he sorted that out. They wanted to charge you extra for a pasty!" But they knew things were tight this time, with Steve Double, the Conservative candidate and former Mayor, also enjoying a good reputation and a high profile, supported by campaign visits from senior figures: "The Conservatives have thrown quite a lot of money at it. They've all been down here." Interestingly, the Lib Dem literature was making a virtue of the closeness of the race: "There was a weird thing on the leaflet – it had the odds on him winning and said he wasn't the favourite, so he was saying, 'I need your vote.'"

*

For most of the Cornwall participants, local factors tended to pull people towards the Lib Dems and national factors towards the Conservatives ("I've decided the Tories are the only people who can run the country efficiently"), with some exceptions: "I'd like to vote Labour every time, so here I vote Lib Dem to keep the Tories out."

Over the Tamar, a prominent national issue, Trident, was also a big local one. Any suggestion that Labour might not be completely committed to a full replacement sounded dangerous: "I've already changed from Labour because he wants to get rid of the defence. I work on the V-boats."

*

Most of the participants had only the haziest recollection of any of the details of the parties' manifesto launches, even though they had dominated the week's news. To refresh their memories, we showed them edited highlights of each leader's launch speech.

The reaction undermined the polite fiction, often heard in focus groups, that people will read the manifestos and consider the detailed policies before deciding ("I'd have turned off before the end of that," one admitted). As usual, the first comments on the clip of Ed Miliband were about him rather than his proposals. "How did he get in instead of his brother?"; "He's not leader material"; "He gives me the heebie-jeebies, I've got to be honest." But the observations were by no means all negative: some thought he had shown himself to be stronger than expected ("Since campaigning has kicked off, he has done himself a lot of favours. He stood up to Paxman") and there was some evidence that people who were deciding to vote Labour were reconciling themselves to the choice of PM this implied ("He's not leading the country on his own, there is a team of people. He's not making decisions by himself").

"Miliband gives me the heebie-jeebies, I've got to be honest."

Some of the proposals appealed to our participants, particularly on the minimum wage and zero-hour contracts, but some who ran small businesses were worried: "Unemployment would go up. I own a zoo" (of course!) "and I'm looking at employing two people, but with fixed contracts and a higher minimum wage I'm not sure I'll be able to. I won't be able to guarantee the hours month on month but over the year I'd look after them"; "It's the same in my pub when we employ people for the holidays. I might only have eight hours for them this week, but next week I might have fifteen."

People's biggest overall question about the policy package – especially employing new doctors and nurses and cutting tuition fees – was whether it could be afforded. Miliband's emphasis on deficit reduction in his speech was not enough to overcome people's longstanding suspicions about Labour on this score: "He's about spending more money. He'll run us into debt again"; "He doesn't say how he's going to pay for it"; "They left that note, 'There's no money in the pot.' I saw it on Facebook." There was also the inevitable feeling about a list of promises that felt a bit too good to be true: "He's saying it as if they will do it all straight away but you know it would take years, if it happened at all."

What do Labour still need to do to win people over? "Prove they're different. Convince people that they mean it that they won't repeat their past mistakes."

"They left a note, 'There's no money left.' I saw it on Facebook."

David Cameron's manifesto commitments led some to ask, "What about the last four years? Why didn't you do it then?", or to think the proposals did not seem to match the government's actual priorities, according to their own experience: "He says no rise in train fares, but we've got the most expensive trains in Europe. Shouldn't someone have had their eye on the ball already?"; "He says everyone will be able to get a doctor's appointment seven days a week, but I called this morning and the next appointment is in a fortnight, and that's under his government."

Some were also worried about the tone on issues like welfare reform: "It's as though they've taken all the non-racist stuff from UKIP and stuck it in the manifesto." However, there were popular elements, including help for first-time buyers, the tax-free minimum wage and, for most, the inheritance tax pledge.

As with Labour, the long list of promises prompted a few to ask, "Where's the money coming from?", but others thought the Tories' record of trying to get to grips with the public finances had given them more credibility on this front: "He was saying we've got to continue on the same path with austerity. You can't spend what you haven't got and you can't always have everything you want in life. I don't think he's promising anything he can't deliver, whereas I think Labour are." Some also felt the Conservative package seemed more modest, and therefore more believable: "They are little things that could be achieved. Miliband was talking about big things that *may* be achieved."

"I work for the Royal Mail, so I got privatised. Now I've got to work for a living, and it's a killer."

However, for some who had felt themselves the victims of

the government's policies, there was no going back to the Conservatives: "I work in the justice sector and I was a cut. I'm going to vote wherever Chris Grayling is not"; "I work for Royal Mail, so I got privatised. Now I've got to work for a living and it's a killer."

Most in the groups thought well of Cameron himself: "When he says stuff, it sometimes comes across that he actually means it"; "He has an air of authority. It doesn't mean I support him but there is an element of leadership." Several in both venues also noted approvingly that the Camerons often take their holidays in the south-west. Does that really matter? "Yes, it's good! It brings other people down here."

*

The Lib Dems' manifesto launch did not produce a great deal of excitement. Most thought Clegg was light on specifics, and they took the policies he did outline with a bigger than usual pinch of salt, given what they regarded as the party's record on keeping promises. People were also doubtful about Clegg's central theme, that the Lib Dems would "add a heart to a Conservative government and a brain to a Labour one": "He told us nothing really. He just said, 'Vote for us and we'll make it all fine.'"

Whatever the virtues of their local MPs, the Lib Dems had not convinced many of these participants that they had "what it takes" to be a significant influence at a national level. "It's the biggest chance they've had to make a difference, but they've … well…" Yes? "Well, they've f***ed it up, haven't they?"

Nevertheless, most liked Nick Clegg ("He's got a good heart"), thought he came across well in debates and preferred him as a potential coalition partner to the SNP ("I wouldn't trust that Nicola Sturgeon, she's got very thin lips").

"I wouldn't trust that Nicola Sturgeon, she's got very thin lips."

Doubts about Labour's commitment to renewing Trident did not have the effect of pushing our Plymouth groups towards the Tories. Most of these participants had voted Labour in 2010 and, for them, UKIP was the alternative attraction. Nigel Farage's presentation of the UKIP manifesto was the only one of the four to elicit nodding and even cheering. The enthusiasts regarded most of what he said as obvious common sense, and argued that by talking about cutting international aid and scrapping EU contributions he had explained how his ideas would be paid for: "It sounds doable and he says how he's going to get the money"; "Not letting foreign criminals in is a no-brainer." But if all this is as simple as Farage says it is, why has it not already been done? "They're afraid, they don't want to be accused of being racist. But other countries do it, like Australia." Farage "says what the normal man in the street would like to have said. Most of what comes out of his mouth a lot of us have said at some point."

But the UKIP leader's taste for controversy was not universally admired: "When he says something and gets in trouble, he thinks, 'Great, I can take it one stage further.' He's like Katie Hopkins." His policy programme also had its detractors: "It's as though he's taken things from the Conservative and Labour manifestos and put them into a package that would cut us off from the rest of the world." Some of the younger participants debated whether the typical UKIP supporter was "a tweed-jacketed Tory who hates Europe" or "a skinhead with a baton".

Even the biggest Farage fans acknowledged when pushed that they might be suspending their disbelief somewhat, given that he is a politician: "If he got into power, I wonder how different he would be then." The point is that "he hasn't let us down yet".

But for those most inclined to vote for the party, "it's not just about getting UKIP into government, it's about getting them seats and a voice. They can build on that. They're shaking it up." What about the idea that by switching from Labour to UKIP you could let the Tories back in? "I would vote for who I wanted to vote for. That's something for Labour to worry about."

"When Farage says something and gets in trouble he thinks, 'Great, I can take it one stage further.' He's like Katie Hopkins."

Very well. But what do you suppose is the Prime Minister's favourite TV programme? "I reckon he's got an *EastEnders* fetish. That's how he gets his idea of what ordinary people are like." Mr Clegg? "*Countryfile* or *Antiques Roadshow*, something soft and fluffy. Or whatever his wife has told him they're watching." Mr Miliband? "*Panorama*." And Mr Farage? "He would only watch British comedies. *Only Fools and Horses*; he models himself on Boycie."

GLASGOW, PAISLEY AND EDINBURGH
21–23 April: 2 weeks to go

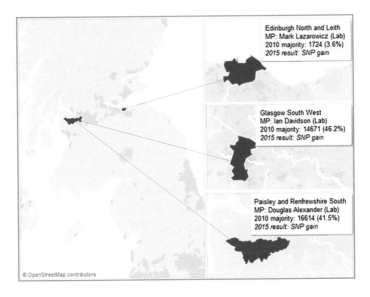

Edinburgh North and Leith
MP: Mark Lazarowicz (Lab)
2010 majority: 1724 (3.6%)
2015 result: SNP gain

Glasgow South West
MP: Ian Davidson (Lab)
2010 majority: 14671 (46.2%)
2015 result: SNP gain

Paisley and Renfrewshire South
MP: Douglas Alexander (Lab)
2010 majority: 16614 (41.5%)
2015 result: SNP gain

© OpenStreetMap contributors

David Cameron welcomed a "jobs miracle" as new figures showed 2 million jobs had been created in Britain in the five years since the coalition took office. A teenager launched the Twitter hashtag #milifandom, declaring that the media's portrayal of the Labour leader was unfair. A Scottish Labour MP was reported as saying that with the SNP expected to make sweeping gains, the mood north of the border was "like the last days of Rome. Without the sex. Or wine. In fact, with none of the fun bits."

*

This week's focus groups took place in Glasgow, Paisley and Edinburgh, where people's appetite for political debate seems undiminished in the six months since the independence referendum. "It ignited something in people … On my building site now, no one talks about football, it's all politics"; "I look into things and listen a bit more. I would never have watched things like the debates before." Though everyone thought this greater engagement was a good thing, the referendum had been a bitter experience for some, and a few had even lost friends: "People were shouting at each other in the office. It got quite unprofessional"; "It was testing for us because we were a divided household. We stayed in different houses on the day of the referendum because he was very strongly Yes; I stayed at home with the babies"; "My mother was a No voter and we fell out about it. But I had to go back eventually because she makes the best soup in the world."

This election also felt different because, for the first time, people felt that Scotland was centre-stage. Whereas British politics had previously meant "anything south of Manchester", people were now paying attention to the Scots. "The BBC news was live from Edinburgh for the SNP manifesto launch. I've never seen that before."

"My mother was a No voter and we fell out about it. But I had to go back eventually because she makes the best soup in the world."

Most of our participants had voted Labour in 2010, and for as long as they could remember before that, as had their parents. Why were people switching to the SNP so ready to abandon the party they often described as being part of their heritage? The answer fell into one or more of three categories.

First, that Labour (unlike the SNP) now seem politically indistinguishable from the Conservatives, at least to the many who said they wanted to support a socialist party: "I've been Labour like a stick of rock all my life but I've hit a wall with them. There is no discernible difference between them; the last fifteen years of government have been seamless. The SNP are the only ones pursuing a social agenda"; "Boris Johnson said Ed Miliband was dangerously left-wing, but I see him as being centre-right"; "Labour sold out the working man to appease Tory swing voters."

Second, that Scottish Labour are, to quote Johann Lamont (which several participants did), a "branch office" of the London party. This longstanding grumble had been brought sharply into focus by the prospect of a distinctively Scottish party having real influence in Westminster: "It's the UK party that pulls the strings for the Labour Party in Scotland – the referendum made people see that. Scotland is different"; "The SNP increasing in popularity makes the differences much more obvious. It highlights the fact that there is no Westminster SNP. They *are* the Scottish party."

Third, that Labour had disappointed them during the referendum – not necessarily by supporting a No vote, but by (as some saw it) "backing the Tories" and conducting (as many saw it) a negative campaign: "They could have been 'Labour for No' and made a socialist case for a No vote, and let the Conservatives focus on their core voters. It seemed like they were pushing a homogenous establishment view rather than a Labour view"; "I voted Yes because I didn't see a bright future for my kids under the status quo. If Labour had said things can be better, OK, but they said things are fine as they are"; "They were fearmongering. They were telling pensioners they were going to lose their pensions."

"Ian Davidson is a very, very good local MP. But he's going to suffer for the sins of others."

Despite this, participants in all three locations spoke highly of their own local Labour MPs. Douglas Alexander in Paisley was "an exceptionally good local MP. Very genuine and knowledgeable." Mark Lazarowicz in Edinburgh was "a really honest guy, a man of the people like his predecessor". Ian Davidson was "a very, very good local MP. When I've gone to him with something he's always sorted it out. But he's going to suffer for the sins of others."

Most did not feel quite the same way about Jim Murphy, the Scottish Labour leader. This was largely a reflection of Scottish Labour's overall brand, since several said they knew nothing about him until he took over. But those who had taken against him either accused him darkly of being a "Blairite", which was an end to the matter as far as they were concerned, or thought he seemed "angry" and was "a shouter": "He's very negative. A merchant of doom." One observation was: "He never looks as if he's really that happy. It's as if it's torture for him, as though it's a real chore." Some did have a more positive view: "I think he genuinely cares, but they are just puppets for English Labour so they aren't going to change anything."

*

The reaction in the groups to an upbeat Scottish Labour election broadcast setting out a series of plans and policies was accordingly rather sceptical. Some of this was familiar from the usual reaction in England: "I would love to believe it all but where's the money coming from?"; "It's funny how in the days coming up to the vote they miraculously manage to find millions and billions."

Others felt that with all parties producing lists of similar-sounding promises, it came down to a question of trust and credibility: "I like the sound of the policies but I just don't believe they'd come through with it. I think the SNP would fight harder for it"; "x-thousand new houses, invest in this and that … It's who you trust, and I trust Nicola Sturgeon more than any of the others."

> *"I got the impression Salmond wanted to be the King of Scotland, but I listen to Nicola Sturgeon."*

So, Nicola Sturgeon. What do we think? "Fantastic. A lot of my family have never voted SNP but she appeals to them"; "She's direct, she speaks from the heart"; "She seems more like an honest politician, if there is such a thing. You can relate to her." Even many of those who had liked and admired Alex Salmond thought Nicola had the edge on him: "He was a bruiser. He tended to flatten people and that's what made him a Marmite figure. She tends to keep people on an even keel and carry folk with her"; "I got the impression that he wanted to be the King of Scotland, but I listen to her."

People also felt she was making a good impression outside Scotland, which they thought was important: "It's good that she's getting out there. She won in a lot of the polls asking how they had done in the UK leaders' debates"; "She was only known in Scotland but now it's the whole of the UK. I think she comes across better to the UK as a whole than Salmond." She also seemed a refreshing change from the established party leaders: "They are all public schoolboy-ish but she has this passion and fire"; "She took them all on and had the answers."

*

For those attracted to the SNP, the biggest appeal was simply that they are "for Scotland". At least as attractive for some was that the party had established itself to the left of Labour, a position into which it had evolved over time: "They used to be the Tartan Tories but they have turned right round in the last fifteen years"; "If you take independence out of the equation, the SNP are probably the same as Labour were twenty years ago. A party of the common people"; "They seem to have policies promoting more equality in society. A social conscience."

*

If Scotland sent a large SNP contingent to Westminster, what would they be expected to achieve? The answer to this question was usually rather unspecific: "I just feel our voice would be heard." One recurring theme was that the SNP would be able to prevent Scotland being the "guinea pig" for unwelcome policies: "When you go back through history and see all the things that have been done to us, the poll tax and so on, that wouldn't happen." Some also hoped the SNP would win new powers for the Scottish Parliament and ensure the promises made by the UK government before the referendum were honoured to Scotland's satisfaction.

Most SNP supporters agreed with the party's stance on Trident ("Put it in the Thames and see how many of them want to keep it then!"), but this was not a universal view ("With the state of the world, what else do we have?") and most did not think the issue should be at the top of the policy agenda. People were more inclined to see the SNP's aim of ending austerity as the more important priority.

However, this pledge was greeted with a good deal less scepticism than the policies in the Labour broadcast. This was partly because ending austerity sounds like a change in approach, while concrete plans sound like things that have to be paid for. But some also felt the SNP's track record at Holyrood gave them some credibility when it came to keeping promises: "The SNP have tackled a lot of stuff they said they would. Nicola Sturgeon was in charge of the NHS when we got free prescriptions."

*

One thing nobody said the party should push for, and very few said they wanted, was an early second independence referendum. "We need to move on. I think everyone's acknowledged that"; "I voted Yes but I don't think you can keep having referendums until you get the answer you want. Apart from anything else, if we voted for independence people would then start saying they wanted a referendum to join the Union. It should be a generational thing, not every few years."

> *"I voted Yes, but I don't think you can keep having referendums until you get the answer you want."*

Potential SNP voters hoped and expected that the party would do a deal with Labour, supporting them on a vote-by-vote basis but not joining the government. Here they would be a positive influence: "It would be good for Labour, bring them back to their roots a bit more and swing them to the way they should be."

The belief that the SNP would keep Labour honest and ensure Scotland got the best possible deal helped to counter the argument that a vote for the SNP would let the Tories in. Some said this hardly mattered anyway since there was nothing to choose between a government led by Labour or the Conservatives ("It's just a different shade of shite"). When pushed, these people usually admitted they would prefer Labour, but most did not accept that more SNP MPs made a Tory administration more likely. In fact, they reasoned, "If Labour and the SNP join up, it's back in balance" – the left-wing bloc at Westminster would be as large as it would otherwise be, but with a bigger element looking out for Scotland.

"Labour and the Tories – it's just a different shade of shite."

If English voters took exception to a minority Labour government supported by the SNP, this would amount to "a wee taste of your own cake", given how few Scots supported the current coalition. But there was a great deal of sympathy for the idea that MPs from Scottish constituencies should abstain on "English laws". With a devolved parliament, voting on issues that did not affect Scotland would be "having two pies at the same time". Scottish MPs should vote on matters that had even indirect implications for Scotland, but "we would be doing our English counterparts a disservice to push things through that didn't affect us".

*

By no means all our participants were now planning to vote SNP. Some saw the party as divisive and untrustworthy and did not support the independence agenda. But those thinking of voting SNP for the first time often had reservations of their own. There were three main concerns.

One was that the party would try to re-open the independence question, creating more uncertainty and fuelling a bitter debate that people wanted to think was settled for now: "They might try to lead us back into the independence thing, which would be quite frightening for a lot of people"; "Nationalism is not a very nice aspect of our society. You see some horrible versions of it and I would be worried about aligning myself to that."

> *"Nationalism is not a very nice aspect of our society.*
> *You see some horrible versions of it and I would be worried*
> *about aligning myself to that."*

Another, for some, was that there might really be something in the idea that by voting against Labour they would somehow be increasing the chances of another Conservative-led government.

The third was that the SNP at Westminster might overreach and produce a reaction against Scottish demands, or otherwise fail to live up to the expectations it had created – either by being unable to exert the influence it hoped (and by no means all expected the SNP surge to materialise on the day), or by capitulating on important policies and becoming the new Lib Dems: "I hope it doesn't divide and create anti-Scottish feeling"; "I'm worried they will get too big for their boots and let people down"; "Can they ever have enough MPs to make a difference?"; "It sounds good but are we going to have another Nick Clegg?"

For a few, there was an additional concern that many of the SNP candidates were young and inexperienced – especially in Paisley, where Douglas Alexander's opponent, Mhairi Black, is aged twenty: "If you had to go to your MP with a problem, which would you rather go to? I'm not against change but I think people might eat her for breakfast." But most either took the opposite view ("I think it's wonderful, refreshing. We need new ideas"; "I feel that they're underdogs challenging all these old dinosaurs") or that it hardly mattered either way ("The policies matter more than the candidates. They get whipped. They even get told what to ask at Prime Minister's Questions!").

*

In these locations, most people were not giving any thought to the Conservatives. Even so, the groups had a very good opinion of Ruth Davidson, even though (they sympathised) she was "flogging a dead horse". "In the debates she was strong. She gave as good as she got from Nicola Sturgeon and it was good to see the two of them"; "She's excellent – genuine and conducts herself well. But I could never vote for her policies"; "The thing about her is that she's true to what she believes in, so I respect her. Whereas with Jim Murphy, you never really know."

> *"I'm worried that they will get too big for their boots
> and let people down."*

And so, to the bigger question, namely who would play whom in *Nicola Sturgeon: The Movie*? The starring role, by common consent, would go to Dame Helen Mirren, or, if the producers insisted on a Scot, Elaine C. Smith. Jim Murphy would be played by Peter Capaldi from *The Thick of It*, or Jim Carrey, or (more encouragingly) Ewan McGregor. Sue Perkins or Rhona Cameron would play Ruth Davidson, and Scottish Lib Dem leader Willie Rennie would be portrayed by "a gentlemanly, quiet person" like Geoffrey Palmer or Ashley from *Emmerdale*. David Cameron would be Hugh Grant or Colin Firth. What about Ed Miliband? "Woody Allen." Ooft.

PUDSEY, ROSSENDALE AND HAZEL GROVE
28–30 April: 1 week to go

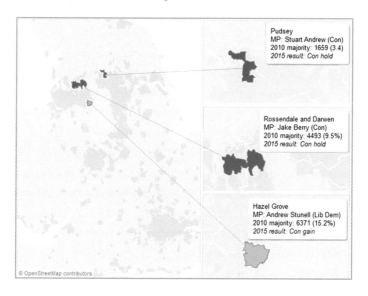

Pudsey
MP: Stuart Andrew (Con)
2010 majority: 1659 (3.4)
2015 result: Con hold

Rossendale and Darwen
MP: Jake Berry (Con)
2010 majority: 4493 (9.5%)
2015 result: Con hold

Hazel Grove
MP: Andrew Stunell (Lib Dem)
2010 majority: 6371 (15.2%)
2015 result: Con gain

© OpenStreetMap contributors

Ed Miliband was interviewed by Russell Brand to counter the comedian's assertion that voting was a waste of time. The bosses of 5,000 small companies signed a letter backing the Conservatives. David Cameron pledged a law to ensure no increase in income tax, National Insurance or VAT in the next parliament. He also warned there were "ten days to save the United Kingdom" from Labour and the SNP. New figures showed growth had slowed in the first three months of the year. Nick Clegg said any cut in education spending would be the first "red line" for the Lib Dems in any coalition talks. Danny Alexander, the Lib Dem Chief Secretary to the Treasury, said the Conservatives had a secret plan for an extra £8 billion of welfare cuts. The Sun *endorsed the Conservatives in England and the SNP in Scotland.*

*

This week's focus groups took place in Pudsey, Rossendale & Darwen and Hazel Grove, two very close Conservative–Labour marginals and a seat where the Liberal Democrats are seeking to fend off the Tories. The doorstep campaigning was intense, if sometimes confusing. "I got a letter from someone in the Lib Dems urging me to vote Labour. Lord somebody." Oakeshott? "That's the one." Interesting.

Some found all the direct mail disquieting. "I get a lot of stuff that looks as though it's from GCHQ but says it's from David Cameron." Do you mean CCHQ, Conservative Campaign Headquarters? "No, GCHQ. How did they get my name and address?" Several reported their recycling bins to be full of election leaflets, but not all: "I've got them in a big pile. I haven't thrown them away yet." Why is that? Are you going to read through them this week and decide? "Oh no, I'm saving them for when I have a real fireplace."

> *"I've got all the leaflets in a big pile …*
> *I'm saving them for when I have a real fireplace."*

For most in our groups, this campaign had never really taken off – the TV debates were no longer a novelty, nobody had been punched and the PM had not been recorded abusing an innocent pensioner. The most interesting thing about the election was the uncertainty of its outcome, which in many cases mirrored their own uncertainty as to how to vote.

This was particularly so for Labour supporters who had, for

one reason or another, voted Lib Dem in 2010, inadvertently helping to install the Tory-led coalition. "I voted Lib Dem last time as a protest against Labour. I couldn't go Conservative, but we needed a change. That bit me in the arse, didn't it?" The problem was acute for some in Hazel Grove: "I'm torn between going with my heart and a tactical vote. If Labour are a poor third, and I vote tactically for the Lib Dems, that might keep the Conservatives in anyway. But if I go Labour, that might throw it straight to the Tories."

*

How, then, will they decide? Some resorted to the claim that they would read all the manifestos – an ambition that was often swiftly modified to "look at some of the leaflets" or "concentrate a bit more on the news". Several found it exasperating to have to choose between politicians: "If you asked them what colour underpants they were wearing, they'd say, 'Well, what colour would you like me to be wearing?'" Some said they would probably decide at the very last minute – since there were still a few more days to go, why would they pay any more attention to the tedious business than they had to?

"If you asked a politician what colour underpants they were wearing, they'd say, 'Well, what colour would you like me to be wearing?'"

Few claimed to have made it all the way through the debates: "I started but then there was something more important to do, like tomorrow's sandwiches"; "I went up to the bedroom but my boyfriend was watching the debate in bed so I went downstairs again. It's alright, I've got my rabbit." Was that from the Ann Summers catalogue? "I meant my bunny rabbit!"

Er, moving on... For those who were paying attention, who had done well? "The woman was brilliant. The one with the red suit on." But several participants also said Ed Miliband had been a revelation, not just in the debates but throughout the campaign. "They've managed expectations about him and suddenly he looks like a Prime Minister. They never stopped going on about the bacon sandwich incident until it kicked off, and now he's like a different person." Even his encounter with Russell Brand had been "brave".

Many still had their doubts, however: "Some of the things he says are quite good but I don't think they're going to happen"; "He's quite emotive and sensitive and speaks from the heart, but whether being emotive and sensitive is right for a PM or not, I don't know"; "He can't really represent Labour, let alone the UK. They will walk all over him."

But few of those already leaning towards Labour said they saw Miliband as a major barrier: "He gets a hard time and he's an easy target. But if he got to be Prime Minister I could live with it."

"When you see the leaders on TV you think, 'You're not real. I don't see you in Asda.'"

One of the things that made it hard to decide was that not only did the main parties seem the same, but so did the leaders, at least in terms of where they had come from. Maddeningly for Labour, people often said that the trouble with Ed is that he is "too public school" – and while that may be factually wrong, it felt true to people because it seemed that "they're all from the same background. Posh schoolboys, Oxford, not in touch with the real world"; "When you see them on TV, you think, 'You're not real. I don't see you in Asda.'" Does the same apply to Nigel Farage? Much as he "breaks the monotony" by articulating "what a lot of people are thinking but no one in power is saying", in terms of his background, he is "as much part of the establishment as the Tories".

But do people really hold the fact he went to Eton against David Cameron? "Yes! I went to Pangbourne and we played rugby against them and they cheat."

*

Impressed as they were by the woman in the red suit, the groups did not welcome the prospect of the SNP having a big say in Westminster. To begin with, they set little store by Miliband's protestations on the subject: "Labour say they won't do a deal with the SNP, but they will, won't they? If he needs to do it to get to No. 10, a hundred per cent, without a shadow of a doubt, he will do it."

As for the SNP itself: "They want to leave anyway, so they can jog on. What's it got to do with them?" The party seemed to these English voters to be greedy ("They already get so much money and free prescriptions and other things we don't get, like university tuition"), hostile ("I've got the feeling we are going to be held to ransom. That's the atmosphere that's been created") and unreasonable ("We don't interfere in Scotland, do we? They want the best of both – they want our money but they don't want our rules").

> *"Labour say they won't do a deal with the SNP,*
> *but they will, won't they?"*

Moreover, if he were reliant on SNP votes, Miliband would be in no position to resist their demands, putting Nicola Sturgeon in a hugely powerful position despite not being in parliament at Westminster herself. "Who would govern the country? I think she's stronger than he is."

Despite this, the prospect of a Miliband-led government dependent on the SNP was not usually enough to deter those leaning towards Labour from voting for the party. Rather, they had to choose the party that best represented their interests; after the election all sorts of combinations were possible and whatever happened after Thursday was, in any case, out of their hands. After all, as someone observed: "The last Lib Dem broadcast amounted to 'Come and sit on the fence with us and we'll see who wins and go with them.'"

All of this gave rise to an interesting constitutional question: "What happens if no one can form a coalition? Does it go to penalties?"

> *"What happens if no one can form a coalition?*
> *Does it go to penalties?"*

One possible outcome is that Labour could form a government with the help of other parties, even if it comes second to the Conservatives in terms of both votes and seats. Most did not realise such an outcome was even possible, and many – including many who planned to vote Labour – were indignant at the idea: "They would have cheated their way in"; "It would be underhand. Not what the public wanted, not what the public said"; "It's deal-mongering, moving away from democracy"; "If that happened, at the next election, I'd think, what's the point of voting?"

Not everyone was exercised about it – but so many felt so strongly that it suggested such a government would have a job persuading the public of its political legitimacy, however constitutionally permissible it might be.

*

One way or another, in a few days Britain could have a new Prime Minister. Do we know enough about him? "We don't really know anything about any of them." Even after all this time? Come on, let's have three facts about Ed Miliband. "He's got two kitchens and a nanny." "His dad was a Marxist." "He went to the same primary school as Boris Johnson." "He's Jewish, somewhere along the way." "He knifed his brother." There, you know more than you think.

What about Nick Clegg? "Sheffield Hallam." "Tuition fees." "Well educated. Didn't he go to Eton, or Harrow? Or was it Marlborough?" "Very good-looking." "Pro-EU." "Likes Classic FM."

Nigel Farage? "The shouty chap." "Likes a pint." "He's like a *Spitting Image* puppet of himself." "He smokes." "Not PC." "German wife." "Plane crash." "Was a City banker." "Doesn't like women breastfeeding in public." "He's got a bad back on him, according to Smooth Radio." "Looks like he goes to the Sunbed Shop."

And David Cameron? "Is his wife Spanish?" No, that's Nick Clegg. "Oh, well, I bet they all get together. Car keys in the bowl…" Steady on. What else? "Family man." "Always on holiday." "Eton, Bullingdon." "Doesn't know which football team he supports." "He's Kim Kardashian's third cousin." "He left one of his children in the pub. But that's OK, I've left mine outside the Post Office."

LIST OF ILLUSTRATIONS